T0061982

POWERHOUSE RADIO

ROUGH ROADS,
RADIANCE,
AND REBIRTH

MY TRUE AM - FM - SATELLITE - AND
AUDIO STREAMING SURVIVAL STORY

KINGSLEY H. SMITH

POWERHOUSE RADIO: ROUGH ROADS, RADIANCE AND REBIRTH
My True AM - FM - Satellite - and Audio Streaming Survival Story

Cover Designer: Nusrat Abbas Awan

ISBN (Print Edition): 979-8-35091-202-9
ISBN (eBook Edition): 979-8-35091-203-6

In memory of
Mildred A. Smith and Beverly A. Rowe

CONTENTS

PREFACE

I cannot deny that listening to the radio as a youth was fun entertainment back in the day. It still is. My love of radio's pulsating magnetic sound track in the 1960s was a strong attraction as I entered my preteen years. Sadly, middle-of-the-road crooners Nat King Cole and Ella Fitzgerald were not my personal soundtrack. These were the singers my mother listened to on the 'standards' music station WNEW AM in New York City. 'Standards' were calm, pre-rock-era vocals. My appreciation for the Cole–Fitzgerald song era would blossom later with maturity.

Mildred A. Smith was born in Claremont, St. Ann, Jamaica, West Indies. My father, Canute Cooper, was born in Jamaica's Saint Thomas Parish. On Bob Marley's island of fame, Mom taught kindergarten before getting jobs as a stock clerk and a stenographer. In 1939, Pitman's Shorthand Institute, London, officially certified her skill level at 100 words per minute.

Thirty-two-year-old Mildred waited in line, followed the system, and immigrated to the USA through the front door in 1945. "Steno-typist" glows proudly from her Jamaican-issued British passport. That was her profession. Jamaica gained independence from the United Kingdom in 1962.

Stateside, shorthand jobs were rare for people of color in the 1940s, so Ms. Smith took jobs as a cook, housekeeper, and child-care provider in affluent homes owned by whites. After gaining a degree from NYC's Apex Beauty School in 1949, the newly minted US citizen worked hard in various beauty shops before becoming an entrepreneur. Mildred opened her own hair salon, *L'atina of Cambria, Inc.*, in Queens, New York City, in the summer of 1977. 'A-t-i-n-a' is her middle name, Anita, spelled backward! Three of mom's two sisters and two brothers would come to the USA and call America home. The youngest brother eventually relocated to London to permanently reside in the UK.

New York City was my home. I was born in Manhattan. My toddler years were spent in Harlem. At two years old, I moved with Mom, her younger sister, and her brother-in-law to the Borough of Queens. We shared a house containing two separate apartments.

In high school, I listened to all flavors of contemporary music radio. Talk radio was another special fountain of facts and fables to catch my attention. My acute ears soaked in the entire realm of on-air audio action!

I'm the only child raised by a single mother. Broadcasters can beam the belief to listeners that one is just kinfolk in their electronic universe. I was there with that feeling, enjoying an expanded family-friendly connection through the radio from beckoning talk show hosts and marvelous music deejays. Each of these kindred spirits had a different way of communicating with fans like me. New York City was a great place to hear the voices of AM and FM variety. Outside NYC, it also mattered, and here's why.

My Lafayette RK 710 Solid State reel-to-reel analog tape recorder was put to good use recording endless hours of strong-signaled radio stations from the North East and Mid-West. The recording machine had a crappy microphone. It didn't matter. The archive of radio media I was taping, that's what mattered.

Station influence on my socialization outside of the inner circle of family–friends would informally suggest, in the back of my mind, a possible future role in broadcasting. Based on who I saw at the time in the industry, the question that cried out was, 'Was this even possible?'

What was the 1969 radio talent model when I was a high school senior? With the exception of African American media, the forward-facing on-air talent pool all spoke non-accented American English. They were almost all exclusively male and white. There were very few people of color. As an added attribute for success, it helped if you had a very deep voice. Basso profundo left women out. I thought my svelte tongue was good enough to fine-tune and develop.

As you'll find out from my early years of breaking down barriers, I decided to pay attention to the external voices of hope coming from all corners of America. Inspiration from King, Kennedy, Malcolm X, and others focused my growing belief that anything was possible. My mother's words reinforced this mantra: "You can be anything you want to be."

Within radio, I'll talk about those Black announcers at non-ethnic and African American stations who helped build up my commitment and motivation to succeed.

Paying attention to early criticism from broadcast professionals was important. If I wanted to be a professional, I had to check my ego at the door.

Here's one evaluation I received when I was twenty years old, looking for my first on-air job while still a college student. Jay I. Mitchell, program director of WGLI in Babylon, Long Island, New York, in response to an audition tape I submitted, suggested these things to work on...

> *"Your speech pattern contains a sing-songy cadence which can be distracting (your listener should be concerned with what you say, not how you say it.) You have a slight New York regionalism which you should try to eliminate - work for a standard American speech pattern, and what regionalism remains will sound natural. Try also to develop more authority on the air - you must convey the impression that while you are a warm human being, you are in control of your presentation at all times."*

Today, speech regionalism isn't as taboo. Jay ended his letter by saying he looked forward to hearing further examples of my work. His advice was encouraging.

Everyone gets temporarily delayed—note, I didn't say turned down—at some point when climbing up the ladder of advancement. All these written tombs of advice from an array of well-respected broadcast leaders remain in my possession. I took them all seriously.

Four years later, the first full-time on-air job would manifest itself in Southern New Jersey. Late 1974 rolled out the red carpet of opportunity for me in Atlantic City, or so I thought. A rough road on a red rug was closer to reality.

I anticipated the debut buzz about our broadcast beacon. Once on the ground, we would migrate from an old two-star trailer to a new five-star showcase. My colleagues were excited. We were leaving a run-down dump for state-of-the-art accommodations. Better performance would be expected in the circle of work surrounding both my peers and managers. Did the new company owners have the right stuff for success with this change?

A bigger question was, "How did I get to this place without cutting corners or knowing all of the right people?"

Before the heart of the story plays out in the pages ahead, you'll learn how a casual attraction to ubiquitous broadcast entertainment channeled me as a teenager into aspirational challenges.

Was I good enough to do this? Did I need to know the insiders to catch a break? Was I at a loss without any family members or friends in the industry?

New automation systems are changing the current playing field, eliminating broadcasting jobs. Artificial intelligence deejays are part of the future AI broadcast landscape. Traditionally, there has always been just one radio on-air job for every two announcers. Competition was and still is keen. With solid credentials, what does it take to get noticed?

Radio has grown to mean many things to different people. At their core, AM–FM satellite and internet streaming are chapters of the medium in which I've personally lived. Today, many young people don't even have a radio.

The death of the medium hasn't happened yet. Audio remains the soul sonic force of radio, as it is for the newer technologies of podcasting and smart speakers.

There's a big difference between performing in general market rock radio and thriving in Black radio. I've worked for both. You'll learn the specifics. My perspective: rock radio is about partying. Black radio is about survival.

If you've enjoyed some or all of these diversions, you are invited to follow my audio journey as I shoehorn my way inside the magic box of Powerhouse Radio.

Not everyone is a broadcast media superstar or an influential communications executive. My true story represents a journey embarked upon by thousands but finished at a level achieved by only a select few.

COLLEGE RADIO CRAFT: WNYU AND MORE

You could build a solid and substantial skill set thanks to a New York City public school education in the 1960s. St. Albans in the Borough of Queens offered me the neighborhood community classroom experiences of public schools 116 and 136. Adding to the lower grade foundation built at those elementary schools was Junior High School 192 in the hamlet of Hollis, next door to St. Albans and the home of many future NYC hip hop legends.

"I grew up in a house where nobody had to tell me to go to school every day and do my homework."

—CONSTANCE BAKER MOTLEY

My mother selected an even more rigorous curriculum for grades 9–12. With no say in the matter, it was off to the private Rhodes Preparatory School. Rhodes, at 11 West 54th Street in Manhattan, was right around the corner from the American Broadcasting Company

(ABC) building. This favorable fact was filed away for future reference. The time to take ABC action was only three years away.

In high school, I was a decent student but not one of the brainiacs who would constantly shine in the glow of academic reputation among other classmates. I had a small coterie of friends at Rhodes.

True social integration was on the move in the late 1960s. Sadly, the racial mix of my high school skewed 95 percent white. However, enrollment betraying the city's ethnic demographic mix did not get in my way. I hung out with a melting pot of cultured Big Apple kids.

One of them, Jeff Siegel, photographed some pictures of me appearing on *The Long John Nebel Show* at 66 WNBC radio in the fall of 1968, when I was a senior.

Music and talk stations were equally shared on my radio dial. 66 WNBC featured hosts Big Wilson, Lee Leonard, Brad Crandall, Bill Mazer, and Long John Nebel. I would repeatedly phone Mr. Nebel's show for that addicting thrill of live talk radio. He got to know my teenage voice and on-air sobriquet, 'Rhodes.' Eventually, Nebel invited me and other NYC high school students into the WNBC Rockefeller Center Studios for a live-hour broadcast to chat with him about the generation gap.

In the mid-1960s, strong, self-selected strands of political ideology didn't necessarily reflect the public identity of the typical call-in talk radio host or their listener-caller. The tone of a host projected the voice of a friend rather than the scream of a political, gender-based, or race-based foe. Opinions were strong, but the zealous cacophony was muted. There were exceptions, but the opposite is true of twenty-first-century USA talk radio. A new sheriff is in town with a big star on a screaming badge, symbolizing loud, louder, and loudest. If you are looking for an alternative, civility is the credo that can be found on public radio talk shows: NPR from the US, BBC from the UK, CBC from Canada, and others.

"Hate radio, hate speech, hate groups, hate crimes really don't fit in, in the America that we know today."

—KWEISI MFUME

• • • • •

I was a very shy guy with respect to interacting with the girls, but never when I was on the right side of a microphone! Subsequently, on future roads in a tough industry, I realized that I'd have to assert myself and learn what was needed to move forward.

As a sophomore, junior, and senior during high school, I worked at Triboro Record Shop in Jamaica, Queens, and as a messenger for the Rapid Messenger Service located in Manhattan.

At the record store, pitching James Brown and Bob Dylan records to different audiences became a passionate personal research project. I was tabulating consumer likes and dislikes in my mind. You can learn a lot about why *The Times They Are A-Changin'* by just listening and observing. Bob Dylan's song spelled out those changes.

American Broadcasting Company was targeted as a summer job after high school graduation. ABC didn't ask me about college, so I didn't tell them that I was already accepted to New York University.

After I completed high school—this is around the time when Neil Armstrong walked on the moon in the summer of 1969—there was no Woodstock Music and Art Fair in the season for me. I did try to get tickets in advance but couldn't score them, so a prudent choice was made not to go.

My "Summer of Soul" (another 1969 NY music event) was spent delivering mail to ABC President Leonard Goldenson. What I really liked was hanging out in the 77 WABC music studio during the accommodating Dan Ingram or Chuck Leonard shows to observe on-air personality excellence (while I was on various breaks).

ABC headquarters at 1330 Avenue of the Americas and 54th Street was just half a block away from my high school. Corporate and radio studios were in the same forty-four-story ABC building.

Performing mail-room clerk duties made for a fun-filled three-month summer. I resigned in late August, and it was off to college.

A full scholarship afforded me the privilege of attending New York University. In the second semester of my first year, I landed at NYU's School of the Arts. Math was dumped as a major to activate the switch. Outside of classes, guess what captured my attention?

Involvement in the student radio station was much more exciting than shooting a 16-millimeter film near the Washington Square Park campus for class projects. I still learned quite a bit about the world of film.

Radio production chores involving splicing silicone-lubricated acetate-backed magnetic audio tape with a single-edged razor blade became a much more enjoyable creative outlet. Cutting analog tape and then putting it back together was like setting up a chorus line of dominoes. The thrill of success doesn't come until the pieces touch in harmony!

● ● ● ● ●

WNYU AM 810 was heard in the NYU student dormitories and in the Washington Square student center. Most of us at the station were amateurs. In this new recreational arena, I moved gradually through my first radio broadcasting experience.

By May of 1973, WNYU FM was also on air, licensed to New York University, using 89.1, Monday through Friday from 4:00 pm to 1:00 am. Fairleigh Dickinson University, which operated WFDU FM in New Jersey, shared the frequency when WNYU FM was not on the air.

WNYU, a nonprofit, noncommercial public radio station, was operated and managed by NYU students.

Before Richard Roth reported (CNN), Mark Knoller corresponded (CBS), and Martin Brest directed (*Beverly Hills Cop*), we were all students doing our WNYU broadcasts at the same time from 1969 to 1973. Martin loved playing '20s and '30s nostalgia music!

Fellow student broadcaster Jon Frank would bring in his own Sennheiser microphone and plug it in when he was on the air! It was not until later that our student station had top-shelf mics. Congrats to Jon for his fifty years of engineering service. He had a variety of jobs, including a long stint at WGBH television and radio in Boston.

Student station manager Denis McNamara, with his rock expertise, would later, at WLIR-FM Garden City, Long Island, help lead the early 1980s wave of fresh bands taking over progressive music radio.

These are just a few of the bumper crop of special talents who were drawn to the WNYU student radio experience.

Thanks to WNYU connections, I had the chance to direct traffic, getting acts on and off the stage for a Murray the K show on May 24, 1974. Murray was one of the top radio DJs in New York City. He made a name for himself at 1010 WINS during the 1960s. Murray Kauffman was one of the first people, like Billy Preston after him, to be known as "the Fifth Beatle" (for supporting the Beatles). Stage-managing for the Murray the K show was great experience for me that I used later in Atlantic City.

Seeing many diverse concerts is a huge benefit of the culture of New York City. On the East Side of Lower Manhattan, it was Bill Graham's Fillmore East. Between the weekend warrior headliners and the Tuesday night up-and-comers, I probably saw over a hundred shows at affordable prices. You were guaranteed to see a trio of acts for a $3, $4, or $5 ticket. The evening show 'Fillmore East Tuesday Nights' was even cheaper. Here are a couple of shows I attended. June 13, 1969: Mothers of Invention (featuring Frank Zappa), Youngbloods, Chicago. Post-1970, ticket prices increased by fifty cents, but not enough to sing the blues for this February 12, 1971 show: Taj Mahal, Leon Thomas, and Roberta Flack.

Playbills also popped up in the city. The Negro Ensemble Company productions downtown, plus the Broadway spectaculars uptown, provided multiple theater memories. I had a subscription to see all of The Negro Ensemble Company's plays during one eye-opening season.

In Lower Manhattan's Greenwich Village, Allan Pepper and Stanley Snadowsky's The Bottom Line Club was making waves, featuring A-list talent. WNYU FM cultivated a relationship with the showplace owners. The station recorded and broadcast many acts that appeared at this hot spot. Student engineer David Vanderheyden recorded many of these concerts for WNYU FM. I interviewed Buddy Miles at The Bottom Line in September 1974, when Buddy was appearing with The Electric Flag. King Biscuit Boy also appeared on the bill. A live WNYU FM studio-based interview I did was with Hamish Stuart and Molly Duncan of the Average White Band.

One of the few WNYU part-time professionals was chief engineer student Mark J. Milchman, who consulted with NYC public radio station WRVR-FM. Mark introduced me to the chief engineer at WRVR. I was hired as a nineteen-year-old part-time engineer / mixing control board operator in 1971 and fired after one year for an incident of sloppy work. My bad. Moving forward, attention to detail was not just a priority but a must!

Never burn bridges. WRVR radio would hire me again as a part-time news writer under Robert Siegel (who went on to NPR). I was also fortunate to serve as a part-time jazz announcer (1975–1976) at WRVR.

"Put it this way: Jazz is a good barometer of freedom. In its beginnings, the United States of America spawned certain ideals of freedom and independence through which, eventually, jazz was evolved, and the music is so free that many people say it is the only unhampered, unhindered expression of complete freedom yet produced in this country."

—DUKE ELLINGTON

Jazz lovers and the listeners of this music on the radio are very passionate. The postal letters would flow into the station. This condensed document (during my second WRVR run) is from Brian D., addressed to me. Brian did not date his letter, but the postmark on the envelope says 1975:

"People like yourself, who are either lucky and/or skillful enough to be delegated power must be always mindful of the responsibilities

*and ramifications of that power. Now RVR pretentiously lays claim
to the throne of being "the jazz station" of N.Y. You and RVR seem
hell-bent on milking it for everything it's worth."*

Page one of his two-page letter contained some credible criticisms.
He didn't like the new trends embracing his music: jazz fusion, smooth
jazz, and disco. The tone of page two of his letter was worse. That's when
the cursing, ranting, and obscenities started to fly.

"Your mindless calling for Pharoah Sanders and Archie Shepp to
"climb on the band wagon" almost made me retch and it made you out to
be a pimp…" (musicians Sanders, and Shepp are hard-core jazz purists.)

Some listeners just don't have a sense of humor! Other respected
diehard players like Herbie Hancock eventually experimented with the
changing times!

It's too easy today to get hate mail from the 'haters' who flock in by
text or social media. Before internet, listeners with strong opinions had
to be motivated to write and communicate by postal mail. Most of the
letters I received were upbeat, even at jazz radio 106.7 RVR FM.

Listeners write by postal mail to request songs, to express their admi-
ration for what you are doing and very often to ask you to record songs.
I never recorded songs to send to listeners via an audio cassette or tape.
They would have to create their own mix tapes!

Fifteen-year-old Pete H. wrote me in a one-page letter in 1982. I won't
include his praise for me, but this is the essence of his note:

*"I'm interested in becoming a D.J. Could you tell me how you started
in the radio business. For example, what college did you go to? What
experience did you have? How would you suggest I get started? I'm*

in 9th grade, about to go into high school. I call you off and on, every
once in a while. But, I'll call you Tuesday at 9:00 pm okay?"

Yes, he called me at the radio station. I often got letters like this asking for advice about how to break into the industry. Many of these letters are still in my possession. It's another reason why I decided to write my story for you.

• • • • •

After losing the WRVR gig on the first go-around, NYC's WLIB and WBLS were waiting for me further uptown. I performed similar part-time technical duties there, but the desire of being an on-air professional was growing.

A shout-out to several radio pros who had a covert open-door policy at several Big Apple area radio stations. I slipped in to see them broadcast live while learning their methods. This was a thrill. The station policy at most facilities was clear—no visitors, especially at night. Luckily, if you called a deejay by phone and then arrived at the security desk, these good guys (they were mostly men in this era) would grant permission for you (and friends) to come in and watch. Thank you, WWDJ AM and WPIX FM personalities, for these evening rendezvous adventures!

One of my college buddies, Pete Walton, was a part-time talk show producer at NYC's WMCA AM, so getting access to see the *Leon Lewis Show* late at night was an easier studio infiltration project. What a "Dyn-o-mite" surprise to see Jimmy JJ Walker as Leon's overnight control board engineer! This was before Walker's fame as an actor on television's *Good Times*.

Other than watching those whom you admire work and taking lots of mental notes about their approaches to the craft, what else could a young person do to break into the radio game?

How creative must you be to land your first dedicated announcing gig when you don't have a contact list full of industry insiders?

While still a student, I purchased the 1972 *Broadcasting Yearbook* late in the fall. This massive (and heavy) printed directory listed all USA radio and television stations along with their broadcast frequency, programming format, phone number, ownership, and executives in charge. Would this insider resource be my outsider ticket to success?

A 1971 Chevrolet Vega purchased new for $2,100 was my first (and only) really crappy car. This all-time 'really bad' vehicle was on its second engine from a junk yard after only 15,000 miles. The first engine seized.

"Sorry," the Chevrolet dealership general manager said, "it's out of warranty!" Maybe this lemon-mobile and a prayer would provide transportation to a small suburban radio station announcing job close to New York City?

Using the *Broadcasting Yearbook*, I headed to the top of the New York State radio listings, arriving in the town of Beacon. This was too far from home, so I passed on calling them. Binghamton was next, 180 miles from New York City, depending on the route. The Binghamton program director was gracious enough to talk with me. Unfortunately, $3 per hour would not justify dispatching an audition tape to him.

Maybe it was serendipity, but I hit the jackpot by the time I got to the M's in the directory and checked out Middletown, New York. In Orange County, Middletown was just 80 miles from NYC if you used part of the New York State Thruway to get there.

Middletown WALL radio program director Larry Michaels (real name, Larry Berger, who later became program director of WRIF FM in Detroit and WPLJ FM in New York City) liked my WNYU audition tape and hired me in early 1973. For a great part-time-opportunity on Saturday and Sunday, it was off to WALL land!

ORANGE COUNTY GIANT: WALL

The junkyard 4-cylinder engine inside my silver Chevy Vega was reliable enough to make the weekend commute from Queens to WALL Radio in Middletown, New York, for eighteen months...except for one Saturday journey. Emergency! What can you do when your water pump blows up with just a handful of miles to go on your commute to work? You do what it takes to get there.

A state trooper on the Interstate 287 leg of the New York State Thruway shuttled me in his cruiser the remaining miles to the front door of the radio station. Probably state troopers are not supposed to do this, but I was very grateful! I did explain who I was.

WALL was a typical, lively Top 40 AM radio station playing the popular hits of 1973. This song playlist from January 4, 1973 (for the on-air personalities) lists twenty-nine of 'Orange County's Most Popular Music.' These tunes were in the top ten:

"You're So Vain"	Carly Simon
"Funny Face"	Donna Fargo
"Me. & Mrs. Jones"	Billy Paul

"I Am Woman"	Helen Reddy
"Superstition"	Stevie Wonder
"Clair"	Gilbert O'Sullivan
"Rockin' Pneumonia"	Johnny Rivers
"I Can See Clearly Now"	Johnny Nash
"Crocodile Rock"	Elton John
"Superfly"	Curtis Mayfield

What station management struggled with were songs of social activism, 'drug music' melodies (their language), and 'records in bad taste.' It didn't matter if music lovers were buying these songs by the millions.

In a July 3, 1973, station memo to air talent, WALL radio DJs were told "Mr. Tambourine Man" (the Byrds version) would be banned.

Even Paul Simon's "Kodachrome," which was played on 'The Orange County Giant,' featured an edit. Doesn't "When I think back on all the crap I learned in high school" resonate with you? That line was removed (and skillfully edited) without missing a beat by WALL's Howard Hoffman (who went on to 77 WABC fame in New York City). Howard told me, "I transformed Paul Simon from a great thinker to a great lover with that edit."

More to come about ornery owners banning mainstream records in a future chapter.

Program Director Larry Michaels (real name, Larry Berger) gave me a big break when he hired me for WALL in 1973. I learned a lot from Larry's programming expertise.

Saturday evening, from six to midnight, and Sunday afternoon, from two to six, were my on-air assignments. 'Take a few liberties under the guiding light of professionalism' was always my broadcasting philosophy.

Radio's music was to entertain, reinforced by curated chatter from the 'jock,' who informed listeners about everything while he or she remained grounded within the bounds of good taste. There are, as you know, the exceptions to this rule.

I once chose to play a James Brown instrumental under a prerecorded local sports report. Well, that didn't go over too well!

Community-based public service had to be included in the on-air schedule during the days before radio and TV ownership deregulation. Every broadcast entity accomplished this in a variety of ways.

To meet some Orange County community expectations, my Sunday 2:00 pm live lead-in program was The Jimmy Sturr Polka Show, 10:00 a.m. −2:00 p.m. (in English). Jimmy is an eighteen-time Grammy Award winner, fronting his Polka Music band. Yes, that's local radio. Mr. Sturr hurled vibrant facial expressions, glowing like fresh baked pierogi, as he offered chatter between the tunes! Pierogi, a Polish food, are thinly rolled dough, stuffed with different fillings.

A live broadcast from a cinematic county fair keeps you visible in the community. WALL would broadcast from the annual Orange County Fair in Middletown, New York. It's the state's oldest fair. Happy kids with French fries, cotton candy, cuddly animals, and fortunate families delighted all. Radio staff would be decked out on the fair performance stage in our red-and-white-striped W-A-L-L–logoed straight-collar shirts. Not exactly Gucci, but good! These are my memories of being a part of the county fair action.

Our regular Monday to Friday on-air lineup featured:

6:00 a.m.–10:00 a.m.	Dave Charity (who went on to WPLJ, NYC)

10:00 a.m.–2:00 p.m.	Joe Ryan
2:00 p.m.–6:00 p.m.	Gene Pelc
6:00 p.m.–8:00 p.m.	News, Public Affairs and Talk
8:00 p.m.–12:00 a.m.	Howard Hoffman (who went on to WABC, NYC)
12:00 a.m.–6:00 a.m.	Jim Frey
John Fisher, Dick Anderson: part-time weekends	

Early in this WALL Radio romance, I found out that you must swear allegiance to honest citizenship by signing a payola affidavit. A payola affidavit is a written financial morality clause promising that you will not accept money or other treasures as influence to do evil deeds.

For DJs or music programmers, it means they won't take money to play records or be influenced in other ways by cash or a gift. You'll learn more about the culture of gift-giving in the next chapter. WALL was the first time I had to sign a payola affidavit. More details about payola are in the next chapter.

Eighteen months at WALL Radio were a blast. Part-time employment was good, but a full-time gig would be much better. In the March 9, 1974, issue of *Billboard Magazine*, I noticed a Claude Hall-penned update that would change my career trajectory.

Based in Los Angeles, Claude Hall was the Radio & Television Programming Editor. *Billboard* was a must-read trade publication. I never missed an issue. In Claude's March 9, 1974, "Vox Jox" column, he wrote:

> *"Walt (Baby) Love, air personality at WXLO-FM in New York, would like to talk with some young good Black air personalities.*

His phone at home is (I've removed it here). If you're interested in advancing your career in radio and you're Black, you might find the talk with Love very interesting."

I called Walt, and we talked. It was an extremely interesting conversation. An aircheck (a telescoped radio show with the music cut out and the DJ left in) was on its way to Walt. Per my request, he even sent me some of his airchecks from WXLO and KHJ Los Angeles (other stations he had worked for). I didn't reveal that I was a big fan who followed his radio journey from city to city.

Luckily, an offer was made for full-time employment, although all of the details were not disclosed. In the late spring of 1974, I was on my way to the neighborhood of Venice Park, Atlantic City, New Jersey, for an orientation conference promising a new radio opportunity in the Garden State.

FROM TRAILER TO
MOTEL: WUSS

The chance to shine working for a 100 percent African American-owned radio outlet was a 'diamond in the rough' opportunity. Little did I know we'd make our own slice of history with this new station.

In the Venice Park, Atlantic City neighborhood, an introduction to fellow on-air talent, management, and stakeholders took place in the late spring of 1974.

Rolling into the Venice Park conference were owners Edward L. Darden (President), David W. Wilcox (Vice President), Albert L. Burks (Treasurer), and John Hickman (Secretary and General Manager).

These Black entrepreneurs of the Atlantic Business & Community Development Corporation (ABCD) made history. WUSS became the first Black-owned radio station in New Jersey. How did they do it?

A Federal Communications Commission report in a 1978 Public Notice Statement of Policy on Minority Ownership of Broadcast Facilities summarizes that on July 16, 1969, rules were adopted to help broaden employment in the industry.

"The Commission adopted rules which, in addition to forbidding discrimination on the basis of race, color, religion or national origin, also required that equal opportunity in employment...be afforded by all licensees or permittees...to all qualified persons.

To meet this goal, licensees were required to develop a program of specific practices designed to assure equal opportunity in every aspect of station employment policy and practice." [1]

In the real world, not much has changed since 1969. In 2020, there were approximately eleven thousand commercial radio stations in the USA. Just under 2 percent, or 180, were Black-owned (stations or networks based on National Association of Black Owned Broadcasters, Inc., Washington, DC information).

This 1969 Federal Communications Commission rule was a start, but hiring practices alone were not enough to foster the needed minority ownership growth.

What would help? A remixed policy of *distress sales* that had been permitted by the bureau prior to 1974, *when the licensee is either bankrupt or physically or mentally disabled.* [2]

Owners losing money benefited from a tax incentive if they sold their radio station at a reduced *distress sale* price. The FCC innovated by expanding distress sale rules. Selling a property to minority ownership was now a part of the distress sale guidelines.

"We contemplate grants of distress sales in circumstances similar to those now obtaining except that the minority ownership interests in the prospective purchaser will be a significant factor." [3]

"Minority ownership is in excess of 50% or controlling" according to the FCC. [4] In the WUSS story, a distressed Atlantic City owner was ready to sell at a bargain basement price.

The US Congress overturned the tax incentive to sell to minority owners in 1995.

Note that Section 2 of the Telecommunications Act of 1996 significantly deregulated broadcast ownership rules. These changes have not made it easier for smaller operators, including Black owners, to acquire media properties. Subsequent changes after 1996 made the universal ownership club even smaller. In the Telecommunications Act of 1996:

> *"(A) in a radio market with 45 or more commercial radio stations, a party may own, operate, or control up to 8 commercial radio stations, not more than 5 of which are in the same service (AM or FM);*

> *(B) in a radio market with between 30 and 44 (inclusive) commercial radio stations, a party may own, operate, or control up to 7 commercial radio stations, not more than 4 of which are in the same service (AM or FM);*

> *(C) in a radio market with between 15 and 29 (inclusive) commercial radio stations, a party may own, operate, or control up to 6 commercial radio stations, not more than 4 of which are in the same service (AM or FM); and*

> *(D) in a radio market with 14 or fewer commercial radio stations, a party may own, operate, or control up to 5 commercial radio stations, not more than 3 of which are in the same service (AM or FM), except that a party may not own, operate, or control more than 50 percent of the stations in such market."*[5]

● ● ● ● ●

Cat hair was everywhere in the 'Dorothy and Leroy Bremmer' WUSS trailer studio. The Bremmers owned the eponymous WLDB license before the ABCD Corporation acquired the struggling 1490 AM radio station in 1974.

Leroy Bremmer was WLDB Chief Engineer, General Manager and Program Director. Dorothy Bremmer was the Commercial Manager. This was a 'mom and pop' operation.

The WUSS staff waited and waited during the summer of 1974 for the license transfer of broadcast operations from the Bremmers to ABCD.

After the $250,000 'distress sale' was approved, WLDB's mix of music and talk stopped. The nonexistent broadcast signal went dark for weeks, reflecting the sound of silence, but not for long.

Soulful WUSS rhythm and blues melodies began to saturate the 1490 AM airwaves on November 2, 1974, the official launch date.

Physically located close to the AM transmitter in a field of brush was our small 'cat trailer' studio used for broadcast duties. Yes, the former owners let their pet roam around the small complex. It showed.

We survived for several weeks in that environment, playing the hits of the day, including Aretha Franklin, Stevie Wonder, and other listener favorites. One mile from the transmitter site, ABCD purchased and thoroughly renovated a weathered two-story property: the Atlantic City Motel. Rooms with sleeping quarters were kept on the ground floor. Sparkling studios and offices were created on the upper level. When ready, we gloriously moved into a brand-new space nestled along 1500 Absecon Blvd. in Venice Park, Atlantic City. Absecon Blvd. is one of three main roads leading into AC and serves as a main corridor to connect to many of the casinos.

Our first WUSS on-air DJ schedule:

5 a.m.–11 a.m.   Reggie Dee

11 a.m.–4 p.m.	Robyn Holden
4 p.m.–8 p.m.	Hy Lit (Program Director)
8 p.m.–2 a.m.	Kingsley Smith (Music Director)

In 1974, I didn't care about the $101 net yield dripping out of my $130 weekly gross paycheck. Making a difference by engaging with the Southern New Jersey community mattered more. This new platform of opportunity captured my imagination. Service was the priority. Through the work of our freshly minted team, WUSS was a chance to offer something special to a starved population that yearned to be served.

● ● ● ● ●

Record promoters would come to town with albums, 45 RPM records, and other charming collectibles adorned with artist or record label logos. These guys (they were all guys) lined up in our offices, sometimes on a specific day of the week, to pitch new tunes for airplay that had just been dropped into the marketplace.

Within less than a month of operation, printed marketing materials were created for distribution to potential WUSS advertising clients. General Manager John Hickman's demographic review told a dramatic story about a shift in local preferences.

> *"The broadcast market has changed as the following data signify. Through WUSS's program design and community involvement, significant changes have occurred in the ratings and ranking of stations; music taste and sound; socio-political thought and actions as well as economic development."*

That was a mouthful. After twenty-four days on-air, how could John back up this assertion? ARB (American Research Bureau), a radio rating service formed in 1967, provided the data.

In 1974, radio listeners wrote down what stations they listened to from Thursday through Wednesday in a paper diary. Diary completion would fall off toward the end of the seven-day period. This is why lots of contests began on Thursday. Today, the radio rating process is mostly automated by Nielsen Audio (formerly Arbitron). Survey participants wear a cellphone-sized Portable People Meter digital device or a smaller wristband, pendant, or clip-on apparatus.

For Atlantic City, NJ, the ARB Audience Measurement: General Market, November 26, 1974, showed WUSS with a 17 percent share of audience increase in the 7:00–10:00 a.m. morning drive time. In the afternoon drive, the share of audience increased by 10 percent.[6]

Hickman details in his analysis of this *ARB* that "WUSS was rated a solid #1 in the Black, Spanish, and medium-aged white market, and #2 and #3 in the general market setting a mark no other station has achieved." He also observed based on the ARB that "the station which had dominated the market for sixteen years in the #1 spot was rated #4 after the first twenty-four days of WUSS coming into the market."

Was this really a time for celebration? Yes and no. If you are the new big thing, you must perform up to expectations to survive. Once listeners sample the hors d'oeuvres, will they be back for the main course meal day after day?

When you target an ethnic community of interest, especially in Black radio, you implement your operation from a broad base of responsibility. At WUSS, we could tell we were hitting the mark when hard-core listeners would write us via postal mail.

I went through scores of letters sent to me at the stations I've worked for. You'll see a handful of these listener highlights in many chapters of this book. Some dispatches I got were unexplained mysteries. We never played Tom Jones songs on WUSS. I do own two in my personal collection: "She's a Lady" and "Thunderball." On February 3, 1977, a handwritten postal envelope arrived from Carolyn W., who lived in Pleasantville, just outside of Atlantic City. Why was I getting a snail-mail letter from the president of the Tri-State Tom Jones fan club? To my surprise, inside the envelope (without a note) was a membership card. The card says "to certify that Kingsley Smith is a proud, loyal, and dedicated honorary member of the Tri-State Tom Jones Fan Club. We welcome you with pride and appreciation on Tom's behalf." There was no expiration date on the card. This membership card surprise came out of left field! Other letters delivered from US postal carriers contained straightforward feedback, including this one from Peg J. on April 8, 1976:

> *"You might direct this little note to your employer: The programs presented on WUSS are excellent, attributing this to the personnel you employ. I also enjoy the updated news programs. Your newscasters are doing an excellent job of reporting the local news, all in very good taste."*

A local news lover sharing her zeal with a primarily music-centered station? Absolutely.

When community involvement is strong, your dedicated listener base should support you. Significant financial support is harder to attract, especially from the general business community, who despite strong listener ratings are often hesitant to embrace 'Black' radio.

General Manager John Hickman writes that WUSS was targeted "to deliver the Black, White, and Spanish audience." Getting solid support from the local general business community was difficult despite early station success. Nationally, there were also obstacles.

The National Black Network, founded in 1973, faced hurdles in attracting revenue. NBN News aired every hour on WUSS. NBN President and Co-founder Eugene Jackson, in a 1978 print interview by Philip Greer and Myron Kandel, recalls that "the network's biggest difficulty was to establish the value of the Black consumer market to the national advertising community."[7]

Professionalism was crucial for Black radio to rise above the stereotype of unsophistication held by some in the national advertising community.

Roy Wood Sr., an NBN news host, visited WUSS in the early days. In later years, Roy would close his NBN commentaries with, "That's one Black man's opinion; what's yours? I'm Roy Wood."

I was in the on-air studio with Wood and one of our announcers, who I won't embarrass. In remarks to Roy, the announcer, referencing a third person, said, "He dun did…" Wood, NBN News Director, corrected the DJ immediately, politely suggesting that the person not include that expression in their language on-air or off-air. I never forgot that incident. Proper verbal presentation and commanding a respectable reputation count.

● ● ● ●

Most stars are respected. Sometimes the glow of a star matters. Falling or rising, a star is still a star. That's why, in the early days, as we planted our flag at the shore, an iconic heavy hitter was reintroduced to Atlantic City via the 1490 frequency.

WUSS retained the services of Hy Lit, a Philadelphia radio legend who added credibility to the budding operation. He did on-air shifts and charmed us all with charisma and creativity. "Hyski" took on assistant general manager, program director, and general sales manager duties.

By July 1975, station ownership wanted changes. Mr. Lit was forced to depart from 1490 AM. After he was dismissed, *The Press of Atlantic City* reported on July 11, 1975, in an article "WUSS Boss: 3 Whites, 2 Blacks Fired" that Lit "filed a complaint with the New Jersey Department of Labor and Industry concerning his charge of racial discrimination" at WUSS.[8] After Atlantic City, Mr. Lit did find fresh opportunities in the greater Philadelphia region. Hy once told me "it would take a nuclear bomb" to get him out of WUSS. It didn't take a bomb. It only took the guillotine of management to decide his fate.

Hy Lit was White. Most Black radio stations are not staffed by only Black employees. During my WUSS tenure, station hiring practices were very diverse. At times, we had white on-air DJs, white on-air news anchors, and white sales department personnel. I even made a few sales calls myself to learn the ropes. To be part of the community, you have to reflect it.

With Atlantic City roots, WUSS's first general manager, John Hickman, created visionary thirty- plus-page documents outlining comprehensive management and operations systems. No detail was missed. Not even his calligraphy suffered when detailed notes were presented to staff. John once suggested that I stop signing my memos to staff with a red ink pen. "Red is the color of war," he admonished. Recalling his red flag recommendation, I've exclusively used blue and black ink pens since!

By mid-1975, after just six months at WUSS, I was promoted to Program Director, joining Operations Manager James "Jim" Byrd to help supervise daily station activities.

This job classification upgrade came quickly. I was ready for it thanks to the discipline and experience gained from previous gigs (discussed in earlier chapters). I can't underestimate what I also learned at WLIB and WBLS in 1972, running the mixing control boards for some of the best jocks in New York City, including Frankie Crocker, Hal Jackson, and Joe Bostic. Sadly, WLIB AM morning man Eddie O'Jay wouldn't let me spin his records, play his ads, or turn on his mic. His take, 'no rookies work with me!'

Picking up the story in Atlantic City, WUSS was my second chance to work for a majority Black-owned broadcast company (WLIB-WBLS NYC was the first). Later, you'll learn how I landed at a third African American-owned facility, WSSJ.

As I discovered, in radio, there is a big difference between big-town and small-town talent. It all boils down to experience and the ability to focus.

Even though I was only twenty-three years old when the WUSS Program Director promotion was earned, my charge was to work with lots of announcers who needed more seasoning. We lost our original golden-voiced hire, Robyn Holden, early on. Robyn landed in Washington, DC, at WOL AM, doing afternoon drive time (3–7), and then continued her success in Chocolate City at WHUR FM and WPFW FM.

I engineered for Al "Granulated" Grannum's WLIB AM New York City show. The broadcasting brotherhood and sisterhood are small. I reached out to Al. He agreed to do some on-air shifts for WUSS. I was thrilled. Commuting 254 miles round-trip every day from New York City to Atlantic City is a grind. Al was a trooper and put in his WUSS on-air time while pumping up the travel miles. In his limited run, Al delivered as promised. I respected him. This older kindred spirit announcer taught me quite a few new tricks.

• • • • •

My best hire at WUSS in 1975 was a DJ just out of the Announcers Training School in New York City. She was green with little experience except for City College of New York student radio. Her audition tape was very good. Miss Rowe was grounded with a Catholic School education, Queens Community College theater-arts credentials, and C.C.N.Y. School of Nursing training.

A Capricorn who learned quickly, Beverly Anne Rowe, 'Lady Cleo,' and later just 'Cleo,' would continue after WUSS to find success at WNJR, Newark, New Jersey; WJMI Jackson, Mississippi; WBMX Chicago, Illinois; WBLS, WPLJ and SiriusXM in New York City; and Hot 105 Miami, Florida.

We had a lot in common: the same sign, a similar fascination with science fiction, avid sports lovers, and native New Yorkers. Our parents were from the Caribbean. Let me put it this way. Not in the beginning, but eventually, after a year, this professional relationship expanded into forbidden territory. We leaped into the land of romantic pleasures. We became more than cordial workplace colleagues. It happened naturally. We were both single. There was no coercion from me at all; I was her supervisor, so I should not have crossed that line.

It was a great learning experience and a boundary that I never crossed again after I left WUSS. Business and pleasure must be kept separate.

After a down period in her life when she was rebuilding her career, I helped Cleo move into a nine-story walk-up apartment in Harlem, NY. She was on a high floor. Those old apartment buildings did not have elevators. Her willingness to climb those stairs after moving in represents, to me, Cleo's unwavering drive to get ahead no matter what.

Cleo and I remained lifelong friends, and we were always in contact. However, she did have some demons to deal with.

It was 30th Anniversary Earth, Wind & Fire concert time in Florida on September 1, 2001. Chaka Khan and Rufus were also on the bill. Cleo was living in Fort Lauderdale, the concert location. With two event tickets, I flew down from Pennsylvania, rented a car, and arrived at her father's house, where Miss Rowe lived.

Shockingly, she wasn't there, but her father was. A few days earlier, Cleo had an encounter with a Fort Lauderdale police officer who discovered substances and paraphernalia in her car. That behavior will get you incarcerated after your arrest. Now I knew where she was. This part of her history wasn't foreign to me, as I discovered some of her destructive pleasures early on at WUSS.

A brighter story is our teamwork together. Inspired by my experience with Murray the K in 1974, I produced only one concert during my tenure in Atlantic City, and it was with Cleo. Under the umbrella of K.C. Productions, we independently presented Philadelphia International Records artist Dexter Wansel & Mars at the Hollywood Theater (between New York and Kentucky Avenues) on Atlantic Avenue on Sunday, July 26, 1977. Regional groups Chapter One and A.C. Exchange also performed.

I sold all of my musical instruments (guitars) and related equipment except for a wooden clarinet gifted by my mother when I was in grade school. The money helped bankroll this cash cow event. Cleo and I barely broke even after expenses. The thrill ride of a concert impresario wasn't for us.

Before Christmas of 1978, Cleo accepted a great metropolitan New York City radio gig to join the on-air staff at WNJR AM in Newark, New Jersey.

Sadly, 'Cleo' Beverly Anne Rowe passed away on April 6, 2010, at age fifty-six. Fred Buggs (WBLS/SiriusXM) and I grieved and paid our respects for her during a memorial service on June 12, 2010, in St. Gabriel Roman Catholic Church in Queens, NY.

• • • • •

The WUSS DJs had plenty of nicknames for me, including my favorite, 'Little Hitler.' Some of my colleagues didn't understand that systems enhance continuity. 'Micro-formatics' are extremely important when announcing. These are the rules of the craft that dictate presentation expectations.

Time, temperature, or relatable song introductions demand structure, focus, and creativity. You can only teach some of these traits. A format provided by the program director that guides DJs on how to deliver a specific announcing segment helps the talent. When seven different talents do the weather forecast in seven different ways, it dilutes the station's identity.

Imagine building an automobile. There is one correct way to do it. Building a Chevrolet is brand-explicit. Manufacturing a Chevrolet Corvette is model-specific. A Corvette E-Ray is trim-specific. It was tough to get everyone to 'buy in' to the detailed trim of WUSS 'micro-formatics.' Some of the older announcers were very much my senior and were not 'down with the program.'

If you achieve consistency, how do you market it? Despite the best efforts of our sales staff, WUSS still had a mountain to climb to become a profitable operation.

In May of 1976, I turned on the radio station and heard brand new 'imaging' jingles that I didn't authorize! What was going on?

Enter the dreaded consultant, making a stealth entrance into the city! Expensive radio consultants attempt to turn stations right side up that are upside down in listeners or revenue. They make multiple changes to right the ship. Often, the entire staff is replaced. Consultant General Manager Larry Hayes and his crew coming in from Cleveland, Ohio, is a huge story unto itself that I won't spend too much time on. After 1977, Larry's strategic approach was to build on stronger community bonds to make WUSS a financial winner. Time shows that results were mixed.

With this surprise change, I was happy to still have a job as an announcer. Langford 'The Man' Stephens began to supervise daily operations. During the Larry Hayes regime, I continued to grow as an air personality while soaking in lessons of survival at the new WUSS, now called 'The Soul of South Jersey.'

WUSS was the talk of the town in my three years there (1974–1977). Outside of the station, The Wonder Gardens along with the Club Harlem on Kentucky Avenue were two social hot spots.

Whoever was appearing at one of these venues would stop by WUSS for a live interview. Jimmy Caster of The Jimmy Castor Bunch, drummers Harvey Mason and Art Blakey, and the flashy flutist Bobbi Humphrey are a few of the musicians I interviewed live.

I ran into singer Teddy Pendergrass, who was alone one weekday afternoon 'stepping lightly but brightly' (that's an old DJ cliché) out of the Club Harlem on Atlantic City's Kentucky Avenue. He might have been coming from a rehearsal. I didn't ask him. Harold Melvin & The Blue Notes were in town to perform at Club Harlem. Mr. Pendergrass was a member of the group. Drenched in the afternoon sun, I introduced myself to Teddy. He virtually ignored me and went on his way not saying a word. Did this mean I would never play another Teddy Pendergrass song again? Hardly. That wouldn't be professional.

In a smaller town, you can perform a lot of community service. I'd DJ at St. Nicholas High School or host the Martin Luther King Birthday Memorial Program at Pleasantville High School. I'd receive public praise for volunteering to assist NARCO, the Narcotic Addict Rehabilitation Center Organization and other causes. My 1976 NAACP Freedom Award plaque from the regional Mainland Branch reads:

> *"Presented to Mr. Kingsley Smith Program Director of radio station WUSS for his outstanding ability, service, & achievement in radio communications to the citizens of Atlantic County."*

• • • • •

Casino gambling was approved by the state of New Jersey in 1976. Legislation was signed into law in 1977.[9] Gamblers started flooding the one casino, Resorts International, in 1978. By this time, the top musical talent of the day, including the now-solo Teddy Pendergrass, would make their way into the casino to perform. It was the beginning of a slow demise for the center of Black Atlantic City commerce and entertainment on Kentucky Avenue.

When artists came to town, the record promoters would bring them to the radio station for a live interview. I had an excellent relationship with all of these promoters. Each had their own quirks and personalities.

Earlier in the book, I talked about payola. At WUSS or at any other place I've worked, I was never offered involvement in any 'pay for play' schemes. I didn't ask for any either. The best organizations have employee gift limitations ranging from $25 to $50 as the maximum that you can accept from external parties who do business with your employer. At its formation, WUSS didn't have a document that spelled this out. Luckily, the record promoters would take program directors to lunch or dinner and pick up the tab. In the 1970s, dinner was cheap! Of course, I enjoyed many free meals. You need to know that my ears, judgment, and research were my sole guiding lights in selecting records. I never added a dog (dud) to the playlist. I never did 'paper' additions. Paper additions are songs that aren't being played but are publicly reported as being played. Some stations did this to help their relationships with promotion people and record companies.

Here's a related incident. My NYU college friend Jon Frank sent me the actual July 23, 1976, wire copy (not a photocopy) of an Associated Press dispatch about a famous New York City on-air personality I had worked with who was indicted on perjury charges. This personality was accused of lying to a grand jury when he denied receiving more than $10,000 from record company representatives to promote their records. Take the low road of temptation, and you often get caught. I pledged to follow the high road and keep my nose clean.

What does the FCC say about pay for play?

> *"If employees of broadcast stations, program producers, program suppliers or others accept or agree to receive payments, services or other valuable consideration in exchange for airing material, federal law and FCC rules require broadcasters to fully disclose this fact to audiences at the time the programming is aired."*[10]

The commission clarifies specifics in other details that I don't need to mention. They do say that "these rules apply to all kinds of program material aired over broadcast radio and television stations." Now you know that a $10,000 bounty to play songs on the radio is not illegal. Failure to disclose to your audience that you were paid to play songs is. Beyond FCC rules, station employers require that most staff sign payola affidavits promising not to accept payments. Social media companies now have similar rules, insisting on full disclosure (to your audience) if you are paid to promote products.

● ● ● ● ●

The corporate board of WUSS was stressed with a cash flow problem due to the lack of local advertising on the station. By 1976, things were getting rough. A handful of times, the bimonthly pay cycle for employees was stretched to three weeks with the warning that you'd better be first at the bank to cash your check.

When the water was cut off at our 1500 Absecon Blvd. facility, I knew things were really bad. After many torturous days without water service, H2O did flow again through the taps and toilets. Management settled their soggy account with the water company. We employees did not want an instant replay of this dry desert tune!

Once, station owner Edward L. Darden warned me and the staff to "lock the control room doors" because a Monday morning sheriff's sale was scheduled. Authorities were coming to remove the broadcast equipment from the studio. Wow! Talk about hurdles to overcome. So it wasn't a shock based on all of this craziness that John O'Day, a morning DJ, exited the station one weekend, never to return again. The only problem was that he didn't tell me he was leaving. On a Monday morning, I was called by the overnight announcer and told that John was MIA at 6:00 am. Guess who did the morning show that day? Me. I later learned that many of the rank-and-file staff knew the exact timeline for Mr. O'Day's departure.

By 1977, murmurs of unionization began to percolate among staff chatter. My management title precluded me from talking to staff about this issue. I didn't talk to senior managers about this either. Unfortunately, when the hammer of station ownership attempted to strike a nail into the coffin of unionization efforts, a person on the staff named me as an informer, which was absolutely not true.

The following year, I was ordered by subpoena from the National Labor Relations Board (NLRB) to appear at a September 5, 1978, hearing in the Mayor of Atlantic City's office to address the allegation. It wasn't fun. Thankfully, I survived. The NLRB ultimately issued a decision exonerating me from the accusation.

With unpredictable WUSS payday patterns, I was in some financial distress. Six miles from Atlantic City is Brigantine, a scenic island with sparkling beaches. I was booted off the isle in an eviction from my Brigantine apartment in 1977. For six weeks, I had to call the Golden Gate Motel in AC my home. Gone in the same year was a bright red 1975 Mustang. It got repossessed. This demon-plagued pony car had lots of transmission problems. Oh, the sacrifices one makes for potential success! I did get that lemon mobile back in 1978, thanks to my next move. I had to score a steady paycheck!

When the signals are right, you know it's time to make a change. Thanks to a conversation with Bob Everland, music director at cross-town rival WAYV-FM, I tendered my late November 1977 WUSS resignation, and it was off to join FM 95 WAYV just in time. Now I became an outside observer of the WUSS chaos. November 2, 2024, will be the fiftieth anniversary of the 1490 AM WUSS launch. I was twenty-two years old when I was selected by the station for my first full-time announcing gig.

"Jersey Radio Station Struck" was the sad headline from the December 3, 1977, *New York Times*.[11] *The Times* wrote, "A strike forced radio station WUSS off the air for eight hours yesterday. Eleven newscasters, disc jockeys, ad salesmen and clerks walked out because their paychecks were late." The report ends with "the employees said they were angry because their paychecks had been late several times in recent weeks."

THE RHYTHM OF
SOUTH JERSEY: WAYV

I entered the majestic Ritz Hotel at Iowa Avenue and the Boardwalk Atlantic City, seeking out the FM 95 WAYV sixteenth-floor studio. It was December 1977. WAYV was the only live FM station in Atlantic City. A wall of large reel-to-reel tape recorders occupied broadcast equipment racks to the left of the DJ as the announcer sat facing the control board.

In 1974, WAYV was acquired by new owners. Following the change, syndicator Shulke Radio Productions delivered a subscription-based recorded song library on tape. The collection received regular updates consisting of "easy-listening, quality music," according to station manager Carl Monk.[12] These songs 'blessed' the WAYV reel-to-reel tape machines through 1976 with a rapture of melodies targeting southern New Jersey radio listeners. Many FM stations used syndicated music services with song libraries on tape beginning in the mid-1960s to address a financial and regulatory issue. If you owned both an AM and FM property, how would you staff both stations and keep costs under control? In 1964, AM was dominant. FM was the new kid in town. What would you do to fill

FM air time without hiring a second staff? You could broadcast programs on both AM and FM at the same time, or could you? Here's the ruling by the FCC that created an opportunity for ambitious FM license holders to run a relatively cost-effective syndicated music solution using semi-automation on their FM airwaves:

> *"The Commission first limited radio programming duplication by commonly owned stations serving the same local area in 1964 by prohibiting FM stations in cities with populations over 100,000 from duplicating the programming of a co-owned AM station in the same local area for more than 50% of the FM station's broadcast day."*[13]

In a later update, the FCC lowered the duplication rule to 25 percent. By 2020, the AM and FM duplication rule was eliminated.[14] The broadcast duplication practice is also referred to as 'simulcasting.' I offered this summary as background. Note that FM 95 was an FM-only facility.

When I walked through the WAYV studio doors before Christmas of 1977, all songs were played from categorized 10-inch reels of tape. On these reels were group vocals, male vocals, female vocals, and current hits. Our format was up-tempo progressive M-O-R (middle-of-the-road). M-O-R was not a 'cool radio' catchphrase in January 1978. We switched to 'mellow rock' as the slogan that best described what we played. Frank Sinatra and Ella Fitzgerald crooned M-O-R. James Taylor, Carly Simon, and Air Supply whispered 'mellow rock.'

I had seen this reel-to-reel system in operation while visiting other radio stations. WALL-FM, the sister station of my ex WALL 1340 AM employer in Middletown, New York, used a similar system.

It was my first time using one. Here's the basic WAYV playlist math. Eight reels in each category with 20 songs on each reel comprised a

540-song playlist. Current hits were limited to 60 songs. Total playlist: 8 × 20 × 3 + 60 = 540 records. High school math wizards will remember the order of arithmetic operations: 'please excuse my dear Aunt Sally.' The first letter of each word sets the hierarchy of the computation in this order: parenthesis, exponents, multiplication, division, addition, and then subtraction.

By this time, we had eliminated the music syndication service. We recorded songs in our music library using a turntable to transfer tunes to reels of tape. With no turntables in the broadcast studio to play tracks, announcers had zero flexibility using this system. We followed a music log and played one song after another based on a scheduled music rotation.

In December 1978, chief engineer Mike Ferriola suggested two ideas. The thought was to sunset this antiquated system. I met 'Mike F.,' his on-air name, in 1970, when he was a student at Stevens Institute of Technology in Hoboken, New Jersey, and I was a student attending NYU. The connection with Mike and fellow Steven's Tech student Ron Harris allowed me the chance to do a radio show on their student station, WCPR, for a couple of months in 1971. That's one gig I never placed on my resume!

Mike proposed a well-detailed all-turntable WAYV operation as option one. Choice two was an all-cartridge system. Cartridges are varying-length tape loops played by special machines. Songs, jingles, ads, and promotional spots are recorded on these cartridges. Fidelipac was the leading manufacturer of 5-inch × 4-inch × 3/4-inch-deep cartridges. Compare that to a 4-inch × 2½-inch × 5/8-inch-deep cassette. Today, digital systems have replaced tape cartridges.

Ferriola's three-turntable proposal (using one as a backup) was itemized for $2,968, undercutting the $5,854 higher cost of a cartridge control room. Mike, backed by the operations manager and music director, recommended investing in an all-cartridge system as the best method. Station owners approved the cartridge purchase. The conversion would be instrumental in fostering future growth for FM 95 WAYV.

Disco tracks were becoming popular in 1978 but were not yet a part of the WAYV music mix. The other FM stations in the Atlantic City market relied on taped music services. They had to play whatever songs their syndicated service provided. Remember, FM 95 recorded our own songs to tape. WAYV surveyed the song pulse of the city, staying in touch with record stores. We had a distinct advantage as the first FM station in town to play breaking hits. By today's standards, it's amusing to read an early 1978 FM 95 marketing brochure boasting that,

"The secret formula to WAYV's success has been a dab of Steely Dan, a pinch of Carly Simon, a dash of Chuck Mangione, an ounce of Joe Sample, a measure of Billy Joel, Melissa Manchester and the Beatles, and a whisper of Donna Summer. Mix well and let it flow."

I don't know who wrote it, but I can quote it (another hackneyed DJ cliché). A whisper of Donna Summer?

I was promoted from announcer to WAYV Operations Manager in November 1978, charged with giving FM 95 a new, exciting sound. Music was slowly shifting to the emerging dance trend sweeping the nation. By January 1979, a special station rate card, a list of on-air ad prices, was created exclusively to sell the hours that we programmed just disco.

We hired Diane Prior, a Brooklyn, New York, native who was working in the Sunshine State before joining WAYV. Diane was happy to leave Florida for Atlantic City to take over the 7:00 pm to midnight Monday through Saturday on-air shift. As mentioned, our studio was on the sixteenth floor of The Ritz Hotel (roof level). Some late nights, deep into a gratis overtime marathon during Diane's program, I'd take a work break by tossing my battery-illuminated beacon-light UFO Frisbee off of the roof. After a dramatic descent, the ten-inch concave plastic flying disc would glide gently into a smooth landing on the sandy Atlantic City beach. The Ritz was adjacent to the famous Atlantic City boardwalk. If you saw the UFO at the time, that was my UAP (unidentified anomalous phenomena!).

FM 95 was hot in the summer of 1979. Our dance music day-part 'Disco 95' format attracted listeners from "all areas, all age groups, and all life styles." The quoted summary is my own, published in the *WAYV Length* Summer 1979, Vol. 2, Issue 1 newsletter. Our announcers filled out listener request logs, tracking who called, their approximate age, their gender, and from what community in the broadcast area they hailed from. Radio programmers sometimes daypart music by limiting play to specific time periods. Certain songs might not be played in the morning drive time but can be played later in the day. For WAYV, "Disco Nights at the Jersey Shore" rolled in Monday through Sunday, 9:00 pm–6:00 am.

Hosts Diane Prior, Cliff McKay, and Ron King helped build the listener explosion. Their programs were designed for radio. We broke this formula Sunday night with Charlie Bucci, a club DJ who played two hours of nonstop disco music recorded at a South Jersey club. Friday nights from 10:00 pm to 2:00 am, 'The Geator with the Heater,' Jerry Blavat, was live presenting his blend of danceable delights from Memories in Margate, a club that he owned. I had opportunities to mix Jerry's recorded voice tracks with production music for Memories on-air promotional spots. 'The Geator' always had kind words to thank me for my work.

Donna Summer, Michael Jackson, Sister Sledge, Chic, and other crossover hits were mixed with compatible mainstream pop throughout the broadcast day to add synergy to the overall station sound.

Listener Abbe B. shared her audio excitement with me by postal mail on April 17, 1979. This excerpt is taken from her longer letter:

> *"Dear Kingsley: I absolutely love your disco cuts from 9 pm on – and we'll keep listening – it almost seems as if I do every-thing to the radio now – from dancing to housework to studying – Thanks again!"*

Arbitron's radio ratings didn't lie. The company now known as Nielsen Audio reported a Monday to Sunday 6:00 am to midnight April/May average share trend in the metro survey area of 3.0 for WAYV in 1979.[15] Share is "the percentage of those listening to radio in the metro who are listening to a particular radio station."[16] In April/May of 1980, the Monday to Sunday 6:00 am to midnight average share trend jumped to 12.0, making FM 95 number 2 in the market, behind the 'beautiful music' of competitor WFPG FM.[17] Beautiful music is a soft-sound format with lots of instrumental versions of pop hits.

Giving away cash is a favorite radio station promotion to pump up the universe of constantly tuned-in ears. You get inferred listener likes and shares by having your fans just answer their telephone with a catchphrase that pays. WAYV used a 'cash call' contest with the hope of expanding station awareness and visibility. Answer your phone, "FM 95 is The Rhythm of South Jersey," and you've scored a $95 payday. To get into the contest pool, listeners sent postcards with their telephone numbers. Contestant postcards were selected at random by an announcer who made the call live. If you weren't listening, you missed your chance to win.

● ● ● ● ●

One person who worked at a station in an adjacent county was professionally aggressive in pursuing on-air work at FM 95. He sent me an air check of his work. As I mentioned in the WALL chapter, an air check is a telescoped radio show with the music cut out and the DJ left in. I wrote him back, as I had no opening. A week later, I got another air check, then another, and another. The entire summer, I received one air check a week.

I thought this was a very unusual approach. There are famous stories about certain broadcasters who have used incredible tricks to get a job. They part the waters of the talent pool with creative angles to draw attention to themselves. You may have guessed that I did eventually hire this person about seven months later, when an opening finally became available. He thanked me months later with a table-side close-up photo of a leisurely attired Donna Summer dining in a casino. The picture was taken by his female friend, who was a server in the restaurant Donna was eating in.

Nothing lasts forever. Even as WAYV was steamrolling audience growth through 1979, the mass popularity of the disco genre was beginning to wane, primarily among music lovers who preferred rock.

Steve Dahl, a Chicago radio personality, sponsored a 'disco demolition night' with his station WLUP on July 12, 1979, at Comiskey Park in the windy city. Piles of dance music records were exploded on the field between games of a baseball double header. This highly publicized gimmick resulted in a riot. Disco couldn't buy the resulting negative attention, even if it had paid for it. Dahl's dalliance was influential in fanning the flames of national disco dislike for some audiences. Before his hardball antic, Dahl was fired in 1978 from Chicago's WDAI-FM when the station switched from rock to disco.[18]

The heat was on WAYV senior management. FM 95 listening was strong, but implications for maintaining stable advertising dollars into the future began to perplex the owners. Would station sponsors remain loyal to an outlet that was tied to a fading popular music trend? Owners Tom Donatucci, Robert McMurtrie, and Carl Monk, along with General Manager Vi Trofa (hired in 1978), wanted to keep FM 95 profitable and professional despite the changing musical landscape. During the summer of 1979, WAYV was sold out of most prime-time advertising space. Would this continue if dance music remained at the helm of the ship?

In a May 15, 1980, Vi Trofa memo, she writes, "during all day-time shifts, no dance-oriented material is to be played unless it was a cross-over hit TOP 40 on the BB Top 100." BB meaning *Billboard*. She also listed twelve songs that I had to remove. Perhaps my local music research was too far ahead of the curve. "Take Your Time (Do It Right)" by The S.O.S. Band became a #1 *Billboard* R&B song the week of June 28, 1980. Eventually, "Take Your Time" peaked at #3 on the *Billboard* Hot 100 the week of August 16, 1980. That song, on Vi's 'hit list,' had to go.

This wasn't the first time music had been questioned by management. On April 4, 1979, Carl Monk wrote, "I heard a new song yesterday by Minnie Riperton, 'Down Memory Lane.' I think it is very much too soulful for the station." Did too soulful mean too Black? Reading between the lines, one understands that Carl meant don't play it between 6:00 a.m. and 9:00 p.m. In 1980, another song was questioned by an owner who heard it driving into town from Philly. "Family Affair" by Sly & the Family Stone, a #1 *Billboard* Hot 100 song for three weeks in early December 1971 that FM 95 played as an occasional oldie, had to go.

I was following the rules, selecting music according to WAYV guidelines, but radio programmers know the rules don't always apply to everyone!

My contract as Operations Director in charge of music and programming was terminated effective May 30, 1980. So what if FM 95 went from a 3.0 – 1979 share trend (April/May) to a 12.0 – 1980 share trend (April/May) turnaround under my music selection leadership? This huge leap made FM 95 the reigning number-one contemporary pop music station in Atlantic City.

After a manager wins the world series or a coach wins the Super Bowl, he doesn't expect to be replaced, but it happens. I accepted an offer to continue as an on-air personality, knowing that WAYV wanted to water down the dance music image that had produced massive success.

Larry Giordano became the program director. I would stay at WAYV for sixteen more months. In August 1981, it was time to resign and look for a new opportunity outside of Atlantic City.

ON THE ROAD AGAIN: WKQV AND WSSJ

The gracious Vita Marie Ventresca was President and General Manager of WDVL AM & WKQV FM in Vineland, New Jersey. Vineland is a sprawling community of sixty thousand people nestled in southern New Jersey's Cumberland County. Frank and Vita Marie Ventresca owned the broadcast properties. Son, Ted Ventresca (on-air name Ted Kelly) was WKQV Program Director.

The travel distance from Atlantic City to Vineland varies from 36 to 44 miles, depending on the route. I had signed a noncompetition agreement with WAYV, limiting my radio opportunities within a forty-mile radius of Atlantic City. The term was one year.

In September 1981, Program Director Ted Ventresca (Ted Kelly) offered me a midday DJ slot at 92.1 WKQV FM. Vita Marie and Ted were wonderful to work for. FM 92 embraced a CHR (contemporary hits radio) format with a balanced selection of golden oldies. I worked at WKQV for six weeks. On one occasion, my relief (the next shift announcer) failed to show up on time. He didn't call. The gentleman did appear forty-five minutes late. The second time this happened with no call to alert me, after a longer period of waiting, I got the Spanish announcer from sister station WDVL in the adjacent studio to track records until the offending DJ showed up. I left. Arriving late for an on-air shift is something that professional broadcasters never do. That subsequent episode of tardiness was it for me at WKQV. I informed Ted Kelly after this incident that I would be leaving. He could now find a replacement announcer.

● ● ● ● ●

Philadelphian James Wade was Secretary of Administration for the Commonwealth of Pennsylvania in 1976, the first African American to hold that position. Four years later, after leaving state government, his company Wade Broadcasting Limited, in April 1980, purchased 1310 AM WCAM Camden, New Jersey, which was licensed and owned by the city. Wade details in an interview with journalist Barbara Faggins in *The Philadelphia Tribune*, September 4, 1981, that "WCAM was in the red and the city of Camden had a $1 million deficit. I paid $850,000 in cash for the station."[19] The format was flipped from AC (adult contemporary music—Barbra Streisand, Little River Band) to "City Rhythm ..." Earth, Wind & Fire, Grover Washington Jr., Patti Austin. Wade tells Kevin Riordan of the Camden *Courier-Post* in a September 3, 1981, article: "We wanted to develop a unique sound, one that would cross ethnic, demographic and age barriers." This sounded spot-on. The goal was similar to my vision for WAYV Atlantic City.[20]

Program Director-Music Director Gary Shepherd guided General Manager Wade's new team. Gary's credentials included earlier success at WDAS Philadelphia. Leigh Hamilton and Nikki Duval, well-known

WCAU-FM Philadelphia personalities, were also added to the WSSJ on-air lineup.

Battling the FM titans with a 1,000-watt daytime and 250-watt nighttime AM broadcast beam was a challenge in 1981. Wade upgraded the 25-mile radius signal with a cash infusion of $65,000, led by Chief Engineer Ben Hill. Might this help equalize the playing field?

I was brought in by Wade and Gary Shepherd as a part-time announcer in late October 1981 but was quickly promoted to full-time production manager. On-air shifts were part of the package. Radio production managers oversee voice-over needs for the creation of ads and on-air promos (now called imaging).

We were located in downtown Camden on the seventeenth floor of City Hall. The building housed incarcerated Camden County individuals who could often be heard from the street. They were on the sixth floor of the South 6th and Federal Street location.

'City Rhythm' was innovative, borrowing from 'urban contemporary' music trends of the day. One of my favorite memories was interviewing 'The Ice Man,' Jerry Butler live, on air one Saturday afternoon. Hitmaker Butler's 1960s–1970s run gained new life in the late 1970s, thanks to Philadelphia International Records. PIR was just across the Delaware River, separating Camden from Philadelphia.

There was a collective effort among the staff to make WSSJ a key destination for radio listeners. Getting into the community through live appearances at relevant spots helped boost the station's profile, but not enough to make a big dent in the Arbitron ratings.

I wanted to work on air full time, but no slots opened up during my eight months at WSSJ. Philadelphia insider connections were slim. GCC Communications of Bala Cynwyd, Pennsylvania, put the word out through a late-spring 1982 *Philadelphia Inquirer* 'help wanted' notice. Program Director Don Cannon responded to my audition tape. WIFI 92 hired me to begin full-time on-air duties in July 1982. I was on my way to Philadelphia.

Jim Wade sold WSSJ in 1984 to WSSJ Broadcasting LTD, headed by Pasquale Del Signore (Pat Delsi), who became President and General Manager.

DRAMA IN THE BIG CITY: WIFI

Native New Yorker and WIFI Program Director Don Cannon was a Philadelphia radio legend. The year I graduated from high school, in 1969, Don was lighting up the Philly airwaves during his days at WIBG, WIP, WFIL, and then WIFI, WSNI, and WOGL.

Don mentioned once that four days after he bought a house, he got blown out of one of his "Cannon in the morning" gigs. We don't use 'fired.' One of those early stations that I won't mention is the guilty party. Setbacks build character. Don was a great example to learn from. Observing his approach to a broadcasting career, I could see that the road to success was long, with many a winding turn (to quote The Hollies).

My WIFI 92 top 40 / adult contemporary music journey began on the 1:00 a.m.–6:00 a.m. Monday to Saturday shift. With the exception of WBLS and WRVR NYC (as needed), I had never worked this shift. Physically, it was a challenge to sleep during the day when the neighborhood noise of New Jersey apartment living hit a crescendo.

Skills blossom when you work in an atmosphere of fun. WIFI was fun despite pressures to grow the audience and build the ratings. All radio stations live and die by this directive. "WI-FI 92" hammered out the contemporary hits with limited DJ chatter. One of my favorite broadcast studio slogans appeared on the wall of a New York Radio facility. "Brevity is the key to success; shut up!" I never forgot these words of wisdom. They were always in the back of my mind.

On July 7, 1982, Don wrote to 'All Jocks': (all DJs) "Effective immediately, everybody shuts up! I don't want you to be creative. I don't want anything but basics; time, call letters and weather. Don't be cute. No adjectives, nothing. No jokes."

Understand that Cannon was one of the most successful personalities in the business and utilized all of his creative charisma to communicate with listeners in a professional manner. On the heels of this memo, I followed the new rules of the road.

WCAU-FM's Roy Laurence assumed the WIFI Program Director seat by the end of July 1982 to fine-tune the 'WI-FI' music selection. Don Cannon could now concentrate on other senior management responsibilities.

Happily, by October 1982, I moved out of the overnight shift and assumed the 8:00 pm–1:00 am Monday to Saturday slot. Sadly, the same month, the staff learned that Don Cannon would be leaving WIFI after a transition period for an on-air position at Philly's WSNI.

Our music mix always offered variety. "Baby, Come to Me" by Patti Austin and James Ingram, "Missing You" by Dan Fogelberg, "Rock the Casbah" by The Clash, "Heartbreaker" by Dionne Warwick, and "Let's Go Dancin'" by Kool & The Gang are songs that jumped into our October 1982 playlist.

At the major market level, competition among radio stations is fierce. Battling program directors create format narratives that sometimes instruct announcers to chime like puppets during tailored and precise talk segments. Marionettes don't win Oscars, but when you are hired as a talent, you are expected to be able to implement this level of precision.

In early 1983, WIFI was about to change. Music was changing. So would WIFI. P. D. Roy Laurence explained to Marc Sugarman in the February 23 "Soundtracks" column of the *Jewish Exponent*...

> *"You will not hear any Led Zeppelin or Neil Young on the station. And we are not interested in Kenny Rogers or Crystal Gayle. We'll be playing rock. Whether it's New Wave, punk, or rock of the 80s. We will be concentrating on contemporary modern groups that weren't around five years ago."*[21]

Culture Club, Naked Eyes, The Belle Stars, Kajagoogoo, and even Michael Jackson were among the new WIFI music core.

WNYU buddy Station Manager Denis McNamara had helped propel this new 'rock of the 80s' format at WLIR FM in Garden City, Long Island, New York.

Radio consulting firm Carroll, Schwartz & Groves Communications and local Cherry Hill, New Jersey, Consultant Greg Beneditti were all brought in to blast the new sound to Philadelphia from WI-FI (the legacy station nickname pronounced like Wi-Fi, wireless networking).[22]

Rick Carroll conjured up significant ratings magic with KROQ Los Angeles using this music mix. He is credited with 'inventing' the format.

WIFI changed. My Monday through Friday on-air time slot was switched to 10:00 p.m.–2:00 a.m. Would WIFI 92 listeners realize that I was now identifying myself as 'Hugh Window' to enhance 'Rock of the 80s' image building? My real middle name is Hugh.

'Moe (Hawk) in the morning' (Andre' Gardner) and 'Mel Toxic' were two other colorful 'rock of the 80s' on-air names used by staff.

'Hugh Window' didn't last for long. When WIFI Vice President and General Manager Art Camiolo summoned me into his office in May 1983, I knew the end had come.

Eight weeks of severance pay in the DJ agreement negotiated by AFTRA (American Federation of Television and Radio Artists [now SAG-AFTRA]) was just enough to support my living needs before landing another position in late June. I am a blessed soul. I have never been without a job since age sixteen except for this brief eight-week period.

PASSION FOR THE PUBLIC: WHYY

Prior to my release from WIFI, I successfully started and completed a six-month training program at the Computer Communications Institute in Westmont, New Jersey. My WIFI work hours allowed me to pursue CCI between January and June 1983. Who knew what the future might bring? This training was my way of investing in 'unemployment insurance.'

Learning punch-card programming with data entry operations was a skill set I never had to use. Punched computer cards were enclosed with paper telephone bills. These cards would soon go the way of the dinosaurs.

Professional radio's allure pulled me away from New York University without graduating. The WIFI experience was a strong incentive to continue lifelong learning. I was accepted to Rutgers University's Camden campus in the fall of 1984. NYU credits were transferred to the Scarlet Knights school. While at Rutgers, I joined Literacy Volunteers of America to help folks of all ages hopefully improve their reading skills. I tutored my students at off-campus city or county libraries. It was frustrating coaching young adults with high school diplomas who could barely read at the fifth-grade level. Many of these early-twenties high school grads had other issues. Family, money, and life obstacles stood in their way. These challenges competed with their resolve to consistently show up for the tutoring sessions and to put in the work required to improve.

I graduated from Rutgers four years later. From 1984 to 1986, I worked seven days per week while attending night classes every fall, spring, and summer semester. You'd catch me enrolled in all three summer semesters each year.

"For me, education means to inspire people to live more abundantly, to learn to begin with life as they find it and make it better."
—DR. CARTER G. WOODSON

In my third year, Dr. Geoffrey Sill, a Rutgers English professor, suggested out of the blue that I apply to graduate school. I had never thought about this. No one had ever placed that idea in my head, nor did I. My focus was completing my undergrad work. After much thought in my senior year, I followed Dr. Sill's suggestion. Temple University in Philadelphia granted me admission to their Master of Arts in Communications program in 1989, and I finished twenty-four of the thirty-credit program before the workload in the job I was about to discover became prohibitive. Later, I did complete one more year of study at Philly's La Salle University in their tech graduate curriculum, hammering out course work in computer interface design and database programming.

Noncommercial WBAI FM was among the variety of radio stations that captured my attention growing up in New York City. During my teenage years, WBAI talk show personalities Larry Josephson, Steve Post, and Bob Fass were regular appointment-listening destinations. Pacifica Foundation broadcast properties were not shy about expressing counter-culture perspectives. Their flagship station, WBAI FM, was no exception. Listeners heard an alternative source of information. They were encouraged to donate dollars during endless on-air fundraisers. Endless because Pacifica stations continued lengthy appeals until the donation goal was reached. Three-to-four-week campaigns were not unusual.

With strong memories of WBAI, I responded to the public radio 'help wanted' ad in a spring 1983 daily edition of the *Philadelphia Inquirer*.

Station Manager Bill Siemering called me with an offer to be operations manager of WHYY-FM. Public service radio is not a palace of high salaries. However, a certain level of compensation is expected. I turned down Bill's first offer, smartly accepting his second a few days later. WHYY employment kicked off in June 1983.

A year later, Bill allowed me to grab Philadelphia weekend part-time on-air moonlighting opportunities, first at WSNI FM, followed by WZGO Z106. WUSL Power99 FM was next. I got bounced out of WUSL after seven months. Getting fired in radio comes with the territory. Much more about this will be shared in the next chapter. Thankfully, I was still rolling along full-time with WHYY.

WHYY FM is the sister station of PBS WHYY TV 12. WHYY was not a Pacifica property. Radio was locally licensed in Philadelphia, and TV was licensed in Wilmington, Delaware. Siemering's editorial vision for NPR member 90.9 FM WHYY was more mainstream but broader in scope than the Pacifica renegades. Bill reveled in his highly crafted mission statements. He had written the first NPR mission statement in 1972 as the director of programming.

The '91 FM' operations manager organized production and engineering schedules, coordinated facility leasing, produced on-air promos, and prepared the daily program log (traffic), itemizing when scheduled events would air.

If this wasn't enough, 'fundraising producer' would be added to my Rolodex of responsibilities. Why is fundraising so important? Listener support provides 50 percent or more of noncommercial public media station income (radio and television).

Just two months after arriving at '91 FM,' NPR (National Public Radio) started a nationwide fundraising campaign called, 'Drive to Survive.'[23] NPR had just avoided bankruptcy by receiving an emergency loan from the Corporation for Public Broadcasting.[24] CPB is a private nonprofit corporation created by Congress in the Public Broadcasting Act of 1967. CPB's mission is "to ensure universal access to non-commercial, high-quality content and telecommunications services. It does so by distributing more than 70 percent of its funding to more than 1,500 locally owned public radio and television stations."[25]

CPB funding translated into a very small percentage of WHYY FM and TV12 income. Approximately 85 percent of station revenue came from non-CPB sources. This percentage fluctuates from year to year. If grants and station underwriting surpass 33 percent and listener financial support falls below 66 percent, CPB no longer considers WHYY a 'public' broadcaster.[26]

Was I stepping into a deep system-wide 'Drive to Survive' hole? No, thanks to listener generosity across the USA. Listener donations during news programs *Morning Edition* and *All Things Considered* helped avert disaster. The 'Drive to Survive' was just one chapter of the 'public media' funding saga that continues to this day.

The radio half of a TV–radio joint licensee must justify and fight for an equitable share of resources. Through six managers between 1983 and 1999 (Bill Siemering, Mark Vogelzang, Brad Spear, Fred Brown, Anna Kosof, and Paul Gluck), the song was the same. Radio asserted, "We need more money to grow." Clearly, a television station costs more to operate. Sadly, the TV station is the priority within a joint licensee shop.

Thanks to host Terry Gross, the profile of WHYY FM could not be overlooked. *Fresh Air* with Terry Gross began national distribution through NPR in 1987. When I arrived at WHYY in 1983, Terry hosted a two-hour daily program from Monday to Friday. The national program is a one-hour cornucopia of conversation guided by Gross and her team of substitute hosts. Popular culture, music, politics, gender equality, and the humanities contribute to the mix of one-on-one conversations Gross has with her guest or guests.

During my first days at WHYY FM, I was struck by the diverse subject material Terry and her producers chose to pursue. I had not heard anything else like *Fresh Air* on other local radio stations. Terry's program reminded me of many of the WBAI FM talk shows in New York.

Crazy things always happen at media outlets. Some activities become legendary. The WHYY radio staff was presented with a note on October 21, 1981. Yes, it was a couple of years before I joined the station, but a paper copy of this WHYY memo ended up in my possession.

To: Radio Staff

Re: Coffee, Tea, and Hot Chocolate Ban

"Effective immediately, no coffee, tea or hot chocolate is permitted in the FM wing of the building. Any of these beverages found in your area will be confiscated with violators subject to immediate dismissal."

Huh? Was this just a joke? Was this just the public radio world? Certainly, it was not the commercial radio world I knew! Cooler heads prevailed, and that directive was trashed.

Working in a 'large' organization with fewer than two hundred people has hands-on advantages. Our Vice President of Communications, Nessa Forman, once toured every WHYY radio and television office to personally collect old stationery, business cards, and other items plastered with an official logo that was earmarked for sunset. Nessa grabbed every offending piece. The introduction of a new logo was just a few short days away. I guess this task could not be entrusted to an intern!

Mark Vogelzang became program manager in 1984, coming in from WKYU FM, Bowling Green, Kentucky. My knowledge of the public radio world grew exponentially thanks to Mark's guidance and leadership. With radio fundraising basics assimilated from Bill Siemering, I began to master more best practices under Mark's tutelage. In 1989, I was assigned as the radio fundraising producer. It was another duty to add under the umbrella of operations manager.

In commercial radio, one is not shy about promoting their enterprise. The opposite is true for public radio. Many hosts apologize for appealing for money during on-air membership campaigns. Off-air is different. When stations send direct mail to their membership base to support on-air fundraising, the messaging in these written appeals is direct, persuasive, and non-apologetic.

Authenticity is a strength valued among noncommercial broadcasters. When it's time for the 'on-air ask for money,' a direct appeal runs counter to some subdued public radio citizens. These can be employees or listeners. They see appeals as forced or feigned microphone-based marketing. They believe marketing is what other folks do in commercial media.

The Public Radio Program Directors Association (PRPD) trained programming leaders in best practices, including raising money. PRPD offered idea sharing, an annual conference, a handbook, and core value summaries. All of these tools, if taken advantage of, can help foster future success. I was elected to the PRPD Board, serving a partial and then full term from 1989 to 1995.

Selling the mission of public radio by highlighting the benefits of listening was one way to build a bridge to the brains of loyal fans. Transactional appeals using 'thank-you gifts' were a second way to etch a deeper emotional connection with listeners. You may have heard them: '$50 for our mug, $15 a month to become a sustainer, and you'll receive a subscription to the publication ABC for a year.'

I enjoyed fundraising. Improving my approach was a learning experience both on-air at WHYY FM and on camera at WHYY TV 12. Raising money on-air for charitable causes in commercial radio is rarely done in a predictable recurring cycle. Sometimes they may do an annual radiothon to aid a charity.

Twice while radio operations manager, I was asked to be the acting program director: March 1988 to August 1988 and again from August 1993 to April 1994. After serving eleven years in operations, WHYY announced that I would become program manager (director) effective October 1995.

91 FM's format experienced evolutionary changes between 1983 and 1995. European-flavored conservative classical music corralled several broadcast dayparts in the mid-1980s. Manager Bill Siemering once explained that no vocals were to be played before 8:30 am.

Since the nationwide network's launch in 1971, NPR's strength had always been in-depth news programming. By 1980, CNN (the Cable

News Network) had begun beaming across the USA. News outlets were attracting ears and eyes. Some dual-format NPR stations (both music and news programs) realized that picking one distinct format would provide stronger listener service. WHYY FM was a dual-format station when I arrived in 1983. By 1987, Siemering had added *Radio Times* with talk show host Marty Moss-Coane to replace midday classical music. Evening classical music was eventually replaced with more talk programming.

Listeners will develop an emotional attachment to valuable programs and personalities over time. Fallout is inevitable when the broadcast schedule is changed. If programming is predictable, consistency builds listener loyalty.

Todd Storz, Bill Drake, L. E. Chenault, and other Top 40 radio innovators built on this formula. They chiseled 'gold' out of 'rock' using gagged DJs, tight playlists, and compelling contests to lead stations to the top of the ratings.

In 1983, *91 Report* was a half-hour evening local news program with a small WHYY audience. The plug was pulled on this mission-driven news magazine so that the short reports making up the 30-minute program could be inserted into segments of NPR's *Morning Edition*. Was this an improvement? Yes and no. As you might suspect, this change was not popular.

Appointment tune-in targeting an endless tapestry of eclectic programs requires a high level of listener engagement and loyalty. Scheduled listening to these programs can work, but at the expense of different genres cascading back-to-back. There's no predictable continuity.

If radio rules the morning, and it does, placing the local news segments on one of the most popular early-riser programs makes sense. For

WHYY-FM, clearing thirty minutes in the evening allowed for the local expansion of *All Things Considered*, NPR's evening news magazine.

Always looking to expand community news on the radio, 91 FM's history repeated itself in the new millennium. A fresh thirty-minute evening local news program, *NewsWorks Tonight*, was created in 2013, only to be canceled in 2018 when funding ran out.

The late 1990s saw technical changes coming to broadcast engineering systems. Reel-to-reel tape recorders were being retired for digital audio software tools. Not all producers and editors were onboard with these global changes. WHYY Radio purchased a Broadcast Electronics digital radio automation system, AudioVault. After training, I worked five weeks in a row without a day off to launch AudioVault. In 2007, I completed additional AudioVault University training.

When I became Program Director in 1995, my other challenge was to work with Radio Manager Fred Brown and WHYY Vice President David Othmer to complete the transition to all talk-based programming.

Othmer was responsible for radio and television. He encouraged the development of new programs. *A Chef's Table* with Jim Coleman and Mike McGrath's *You Bet Your Garden* are two-hour-long productions that I helped tweak as Program Director. The line producers of these shows also deserve lots of developmental credit.

Daily, short, two-minute audio features were a staple of an earlier age of radio. Today, sports talk radio will often use short audio modules to express editorial commentary about sports news. During the late 1990s, I was open-minded enough to program selected syndicated standouts from this audio feature genre where they made the most sense. A modular, local, home-grown two-minute feature was Dr. Myrna Shure's Parenting

Tips. These featurettes were offered as a sequel to a series of one-hour *Raising a Thinking Child* (Myrna's parenting book) specials.

By 1998, WHYY's David Othmer had sketched a mental blueprint to work with WRTI FM, Temple University's jazz-classical station, and WXPN, the University of Pennsylvania's eclectic FM music purveyor. David proposed a plan to further fine-tune the 91 FM broadcast schedule. His idea would expand the XPN and RTI talent pools.

WHYY FM's folk host, Gene Shay, would move to WXPN. 91 FM's jazz host, Bob Perkins, would migrate to WRTI. The plan was implemented. Talk-based programming would replace WHYY FM's Sunday afternoon opera with host Wayne Conner.

These changes were a seismic shift for legacy public radio station WHYY FM.

Public acceptance of these controversial moves was echoed by allegiances to either music or talk. The *Philadelphia Inquirer* published a dual op-ed, "Where has all the radio gone?" on Monday, January 12, 1998.[27] I authored part of this dual-opinion piece: "*Stations must explain themselves to listeners in times of change.*" Here's a small excerpt of what I wrote.

> *"Radio, more than any other electronic medium, has the endearing capacity to cement an emotional bond with a listener. The music, conversation, dialogue and personalities leave an indelible mark. When a broadcast facility sets out to accomplish specific goals and, in the process, breaks the trust between station and audience, listeners and viewers become justifiably upset."*

For listener-supported public media—radio, television, online, and podcasts—there's an even closer connection thanks to financial contributions from the active users of the service. I continued . . .

"The nature of change in broadcasting may sometimes appear to violate listeners' trust and loyalty. That is why when radio stations change, they ought to explain themselves."

Competitive reasons may dissuade programming gurus from telegraphing some strategic moves in advance, especially when earth-shattering changes are coming. But a level of authentic transparency is important. Managers can take advantage of an open window through which their airborne gusts of vocal explanations influence listener expectations to build trust.

A different opinion popped out of the newspaper pages in this two-person commentary. Writer Mark Rohland countered, "WHYY has canceled the past - and all my reasons for listening." Mark penned:

"I didn't stop listening to Philadelphia's chief public radio station, WHYY, because it stopped broadcasting classical music seven years ago. Neither did I stop because the station has responded cravenly to federal funding cuts with blatant marketing strategies that undercut its claim to be commercial-free . . . What did make me change my digital settings from WHYY for good instead was a realization. Brooding over whether anything but my own nostalgia justified my distaste for the changes; I recognized that my unease stemmed from the disappearance of programming I would have wanted to listen to as a child."

He continued to amplify this theme in his half of the opinion piece. To understand the passion for preserving the past voiced by Mark's perspective, you must understand that limited listener options existed in 1998 radio. There were not that many available alternatives.

New competition was about to come from online pioneers. Streamers Live365 and Pandora started at about the same time. Live365 started in 1999, and Pandora formed in 2000. Pandora launched in 2005. By 2006, Spotify was in the game. (Much more about streaming is in the Live365 chapter.)

Everyone operating in the public eye knows that some people will not be happy with change.

● ● ● ● ●

In 1998, I purchased a split-level house in New Jersey, not knowing that by January 2000, I would enter a new frontier. One evening during a November 1999 WHYY broadcast of NPR's *All Things Considered*, host Robert Siegel announced that 'ATC' Senior Producer Margaret Low would be leaving the program to head up NPR's satellite radio division. I didn't know anything about satellite radio. I did reason that it would be fascinating to learn about and explore this new axis of AM – FM – Sputnik media. Sputnik was the first artificial satellite launched by the Soviet Union in 1957.

Margaret contacted me within days of receiving my application to join NPR. After several interviews, I was hired as one of two satellite radio program directors along with Andrew Morrell. Online, I located an Alexandria, Virginia, studio apartment. This would be my weekday home for the next seventeen and a half years. But keeping the NJ house turned out to be a smart decision. I commuted back to New Jersey every weekend, escaping the daily intensity of Washington, DC. Goodbye, WHYY, in January 2000. Hello, NPR in February 2000.

COMMERCIAL RADIO FAST LANE: WSNI, WZGO, AND WUSL

C ommercial radio can operate like a circus. The ringmaster is the Federal Communications Commission. Stations follow FCC guidelines to build up a boatload of listeners. AM, FM, and TV properties charge ahead to generate revenue.

Competition in large markets is brutal. Anything goes to attract and retain nonstop listening or viewing. During the 1980s, Philadelphia was the fifth largest market in the USA. I hopped on board Philly's 104.5 FM WSNI in September 1984 thanks to another opportunity offered by Operations Manager Don Cannon. Saturday and Sunday, 12:00 a.m.–6:00 a.m. on-air, was my part-time charge.

There are a lot of reasons why some stations get to the top of the ratings and stay there. It might be broadcast dial location, transmitter power output, on-air personalities, perpetual contests, or the music. Certain performers may grant 'most favored nation' status to a popular station for exclusive interviews.

WSNI was in the mix, slogging it out for a top spot against market leaders WMGK Magic 102 and B101 FM. We played contemporary hits along with some old gold. Too bad Olivia Newton John and America had hit song titles with the word 'magic' in them. WSNI rules of engagement forbade mentioning these song titles when played (if we played them). One of my favorite 1985 memos to the entire air staff was from Program Director Paul Tyler, who counseled, "Please do not mention the title of Madonna's latest song on the air ("Like a Virgin"). DO NOT MENTION THAT ON AIR . . ."

These notes are not unusual from program directors. Spelling out and bellowing bylaws were considered best practices for business. The specificity of directives telling you how to say what to say was endless. PD team leaders hoped that micro-formatic directions would enhance possible ratings success. "Just don't make the station sound too 'hip' or too 'wimpy'" is another one of my Tyler favorites. This guidance was part of a decree telling us how to pre-promote music sweeps (back-to-back songs). We were told to pick "the right artists" (examples were given). No disrespect to Paul. He was a pleasure to work with providing ample feedback for my growth.

From 1983 to 1985, I carried the Saturday and Sunday WSNI flag forward, also attending Rutgers University in the evening while working full-time weekdays at WHYY FM. This schedule meant two full years of work with just a handful of days off (thanks to the very accommodating WSNI).

Kudos to radio legend Dan Ingram, a familiar face whom I talked about in a previous chapter. Dan was the chairman of AFTRA's National Disc Jockey Caucus in 1985. I was happy to see him again when he met with the WSNI Philadelphia staff to lend his support for contract negotiations. AFTRA is now the SAG-AFTRA union.

I had the chance to get off of overnight work by jumping to WZGO Z106 part-time in July 1985. Inside the small community of on-air communicators, you'll often find familiar faces when cycling into a new station in the same city. Z106 was no different. Andre' Gardner was there. We both put in previous time concurrently at FM outlets WIFI 92 and 104.5 WSNI.

Once again at Z106, I was playing the contemporary hits of the day. Among the four Philly FM music stations I worked for on-air, Z106 was the most fun. (The story of the fourth station is still to come.) My malleable presentation style worked well for delivering Z106's sonic sound of hit music. WZGO battled WCAU-FM 98, among other competitors.

In early 1986, Z106 management announced that consultant Mike Joseph was coming back to town for a WZGO reboot. Joseph used his 'hot hits' format to reinvent WCAU-FM in 1981. With change coming, the Z106 on-air staff could reapply for positions before Joseph walked in the door.

'Hot hits' Mike was known for his 1967 Philly ratings war victory at WFIL over competitor WIBG.[28]

Consultants always want their own people, so I chose not to overextend my welcome and reapply for my job. It was prudent to escape before the guillotine fell. Popular music was morphing under the influence of hip-hop. The timing for a change of venue felt right. I jumped ship, waving goodbye to my WZGO friends, and headed crosstown to WUSL Power 99fm for another part-time on-air gig.

In 1986, the sound of hip-hop was moving from the streets to radio speakers. Philly's Power 99fm featured *Street Beat* with host Lady B as the place for rap. I landed at WUSL with a Saturday evening on-air shift adjacent to *Street Beat*. Rhythm and blues remained the focal point of the music flow, with hip-hop inching into an expanding playlist. The Power 99fm October 10, 1986, 'Power Plays' top twenty-five songs list included three hip-hop contributions: "One Love" by Whodini, "Eric B for President" by Eric B, and "Walk This Way" by Run D.M.C. Note that the name "Eric B for President" was a licensing error. "Eric B Is President" is the correct title.

Radio DJs follow a musical clock specifying what classification of song is played at what time within an hour. Power 99 fm's sonic beat pumped out 'thirty-minute commercial-free supersets' in rotating clock positions within most hours. That is, in one hour the superset might start at eleven minutes past. The next hour we might jump into it at twenty-two minutes past (ending the sweep at fifty-two past).

Announcers were lively but not frenetic. This approach, mixing newer music with measured DJ prose, built a loyal and younger audience than competitor WDAS-FM.

Most radio stations try to have visibility in their communities. WUSL did a great job using on-air personalities to pound the pavements of local Philadelphia neighborhoods. We'd announce where we'd be, then walk through the community handing out swag branded with the radio station logo. One of my favorite Power 99fm adventures was cruising on foot through sections of Camden, New Jersey, gifting residents on the street with good stuff.

Other grassroots campaign activities to help solve serious community problems were always visible on and off air, led by our civic and public affairs team.

Did you know that most successful radio announcers don't just show up for work, flip on a microphone, and dive into their presentation? Show preparation is key. Getting to the broadcast center an hour before airtime was always part of my regimen. I'd write my own weather in simple language based on the National Weather Service forecast. Show planning included mapping out local stories of interest, including sports scores. These elements would be dropped into brief talk segments.

To support individual preparation, Power 99fm had lots of informational lists to use. All the high schools were on one document. School spirit shout-outs could be liberally mentioned from 6:00 am to 8:00 am or 3:00 pm to midnight. Delaware Valley colleges and universities in the Philadelphia region were highlighted on several printed pages. Comprehensive industry, city, road, street, interstate, and community location data was compiled in complete lists for our use. Paper ruled. There was no Internet. Creative research delivered benefits.

Power 99fm was a good example of 1980s 'urban radio.' The urban tag was a euphemism for 'Black.' Marketers invented the tag to make it easier to sell station ads to white megacorporations and mom-and-pop businesses. Why? There was a history of resistance in the commercial ad world to radio stations with large Black audiences. It didn't matter that African American consumers liberally used general market products. Getting these advertisers on board was a tough sell, even if station ratings were successful.

'Urban' radio primarily played Black music. Listeners knew what was being presented. However, an identity crisis existed, as scrutinized by broadcast industry professionals.

I rolled on at Power 99fm until November 1986. By surprise, Program Director Tony Quartarone placed an unexpected telephone call to me. His timing was reasonable, as I wasn't on the air or at the station. "Your tenure is over." I'm paraphrasing. He was respectful. Tony Q got right to the point. Getting fired in broadcasting is a badge of honor. You really haven't made it until you've risen like the Phoenix to reappear somewhere else. This was the third time I was on the station chopping block. One offending employer, WRVR FM in New York City, as I've mentioned earlier, rehired me years later as a part-time weekday news writer and as a weekend newscaster and jazz host.

Often, you are told, "You don't fit into our future direction." In the end, that's the exact phrase WIFI Vice President and General Manager Art Camiolo used in 1983.

As I always had two or three jobs at the same time, except for one two-month period in 1983, my 1986 release from Power 99fm allowed me to concentrate on my final two years at Rutgers University. Thankfully, the WHYY FM job was going well. When I graduated from Rutgers in 1988, WHYY rewarded me with a nice big salary bump.

CREATING MY OWN SPACE:
POWERHOUSE RADIO ONLINE

Live365 is an online audio streaming service created in 1999. Competitor Pandora was founded in 2000 and launched in 2005.

Music streaming to a mobile device was still a novelty at the dawn of the new millennium. Spotify joined the digital music revolution by 2006. The digital file sharer Napster, created in 1999, is now just a fleeting music memory.

Today's smart speakers are a convenient contemporary reincarnation of digital streaming circa 2005. These new devices use wireless technology to make connecting to audio streams simple.

With a huge library of songs and personal knowledge about the tracks, I joined the 'radio revolution' rebel Live365 in 2000. By 2001, I was ready to launch my own dedicated twenty-four-hour online streaming channel. Note that Live365, including my feed, unexpectedly shut down in January 2016. Live365 did return in 2018. I chose not to come back.

Within a sixteen-year period, here's how I was able to grow my channel to become the number one rhythm and blues Live365 outlet based on listener hours per month. 'Classic soul' was my channel's sub-genre. It coexisted among the many available R&B stations. We do get a little technical in this chapter, but it will help advance the story while explaining exactly how I achieved the growth. Online streamers and podcasters might find some inspiration from the models I used. You may benefit from some of these ideas.

Listeners of many successful AM and FM stations receive weak broadcast signals. Low-quality radio receivers could be responsible. Another factor is the distance from the radio to the broadcast tower. In cities, FM signals can reflect off of tall buildings, causing radio 'multipath,' a distortion heard in the receiver's speaker system.

Passionate lovers of a unique format will support a service they love and trust even if the sound quality is marginal or challenged by technical hurdles.

Possessing this knowledge, I started Powerhouse Radio on Live365 using low-bandwidth MP3 music files. Really low. Sixteen thousand kilohertz mono. Despite selecting 'AM' sound quality, listeners never complained. Maybe it was the novelty? Maybe it was my music selection? Perhaps it was my skill at mixing artists, tempos, genres, and genders based on my many years of professional radio experience. I do know that after a couple of years of airing ads on the channel, I decided to go commercial-free. This change definitely helped build an audience.

Powerhouse Radio was automated using Live365's proprietary software tools. I structured the sequence of songs in a specific order, track by track. Each music playlist contained twenty-seven to thirty-six hours of songs in a fixed order. My favorite playlist length was twenty-nine hours, thirty minutes.

In the early 2000s, most online music listening was done at the work-place using desktop computers. Here's how I served that audience. The Live365 server would advance the music forward five hours or more each day within my playlist (based on a twenty-four-hour clock). Listeners would hear different songs at different times during the 9:00 a.m.–5:00 p.m. workday. The rotation would always move forward by five hours or more, depending on the length of the specific playlist. Listeners tuning in at the same time on different days would not hear the same songs. Here's an example: A twenty-nine-hour playlist starts at 6:00 a.m. on Monday. On Tuesday, the playlist ends at 11:00 a.m. and restarts. Note that this is twenty-nine hours later. This is why twenty-seven-to-thirty-six-hour playlists worked so well.

Using this tactic made it hard for anyone to figure out a pattern of repetition. I used a library of nearly forty different playlists. These instruction lists were placed into rotation once per week. Saturday evening was my favorite time to start the next playlist using Live365's scheduling automation. This regular process was low-maintenance. I'd update several tracks in each playlist as needed to keep things fresh. All music was culled from my own personal library.

I used two turntables in my home studio to digitize my collection of albums and 45 RPM vinyl singles. For more variety, I would also use a couple of CD players to digitize tracks from CDs and occasionally down-load songs from iTunes. All music from the beginning of the Powerhouse Radio project was recorded on a computer in monaural wav format, then converted to MP3 files. Some vinyl and digital tracks were burned to CD for archiving.

By 2008, it was clear that I needed to adopt stereo and swap the 'AM' sound for 'FM' clarity. On the internet, online streaming bandwidth was maturing into a more affordable service. In 2001, server-based file storage was costly. Live365 reflected this reality. Using lower-bandwidth music files to build a large library of songs made sense. The plan: smaller music files, less storage space, lower cost. By 2008, file storage allocations had become larger and cheaper. How did I rebuild the repository of songs to boast brighter, sharper, and smoother frequencies?

REBUILDING THE LIBRARY

The first step was to rerecord the music library by digitizing approximately two thousand songs into the Red Book wav stereo format. Red Book is a compact disc standard defined by Sony and Philips. Music is recorded in stereo at a frequency of 44.1 kilohertz in a 16-bit configuration. From the uncompressed WAV file, a separate compressed MP3 file can be created. Software apps allow MP3 files to be created using different compression levels without sacrificing too much of the audio quality. The trade-off is file size. Thankfully, MP3 music files are much smaller than their uncompressed WAV counterparts. My rerecording process took a couple of years. Failing to record using Red Book WAV stereo from the very beginning was a big mistake.

My approach to recording music was straightforward, but preparing the tracks for MP3 playback was not. I believed in 'normalizing,' that is, raising (or lowering) the volume of each song by hand using Cool Edit Pro Windows digital audio software. This was done after a song was recorded. Cool Edit was eventually acquired by Adobe and is now called Adobe Audition. In Cool Edit, I would adjust the volume of all songs to the same playback level. Doing this is tricky. Physical analog and digital records have inconsistent sound volumes. I used the song "Shake It Up Tonight" by Cheryl Lynn, chosen at random, as my audio volume barometer. Trusting your ears is always a good thing. All songs were matched to this arbitrary sonic threshold. Sometimes viewing the ping and flutter of sound volume meters in digital audio software can result in inaccurate recording levels.

Even more work was required to meet my standards after normalizing tracks. Songs with low beginnings were boosted again. Just the specific low pass section at the start of the song was boosted a second time. All tracks were polished off by fine-tuning a super tight, natural-sounding custom song-end fade. This step wasn't mandatory if a tune had a 'cold' ending with no fade.

The Live365 automation system did not include cross-fading. That's the ability to overlap the end of one record by a few seconds over the beginning of the next song. My hands-on approach to crafting consistent music levels circumvented the limitations of Live365's automation.

AM and FM stations pass their broadcast signal through 'magic' electronic boxes before exiting the studio and arriving at the radio transmitter. These lightning-fast digital devices instantly lower or raise audio levels to a standard benchmark. The sound of audio being compressed results when this technology is pushed to its limit. Compression artifacts can be annoying to listen to on a radio station when the technology is tuned to extremes. For AM or FM, you'll hear a quick up-and-down audio swoosh when there is a pause in the DJ's or news announcer's dialog. High-energy rock radio uses this digital equipment to create a very compressed on-air sound. Why? Because the original top forty AM radio stations sounded this way. FM just followed tradition. Some feel this technical touch makes the audio chain from studio to radio more exciting to listen to.

Hand-tweaking all of the Powerhouse Radio tracks mimicked some of these 'magic' box techniques. But that's not all that was done. Many tracks were skillfully remixed. My favorite was Prince's "Sexy M.F." If you sampled my version, you'd never know anything was done to the song (except if you were waiting to hear the four-letter words).

Another favorite trick was to play blatant curse words backwards in the track by using fancy editing. The song melody would not miss a beat while the listeners were entertained! On just two occasions, I used a bleep tone to cover profanity. The award winners were Millie Jackson's live version of "If Loving You Is Wrong, I Don't Want to Be Right" and Clarence 'Blowfly' Reid's "Rapp Dirty." The goal was to keep the stream cutting-edge for adults but clean enough for consumption by general audiences. Remember, lots of people were listening in the workplace with and without headphones or earbuds.

Additional editorial decisions shaped my Powerhouse Radio sound. There was a 6-minute limit placed on certain extended dance tracks. This wasn't done often. It depended on how good the song was. Lots of these tracks might run eight or nine minutes.

Our audience preferred album-length versions over shortened record company singles. All rules have exceptions. Even ours. Some short and long versions of the same song were played at different times in the week based on what my thematic theater of the mind was trying to create. However, we didn't play the shorter song versions very often.

Royalty-free production music libraries were used to create image-building jingles. These short four-second to fifteen-second voice-over music brand-building spots reinforced the aural character of Powerhouse Radio. I used them to buffer jarring music segues. Normally, four to six or more songs would be played back-to-back without any talking. A recorded tagline over music in these short image spots bridged song-to-song tempo transitions. Think slow to fast, fast to slow, or other combinations. The beginning and end of the music in these jingles would match the tempos of the adjacent songs. They were produced this way by the music production companies. I added voiced station identification elements on top of these 'music button' jingles. To promote a station blog, newsletter, and website, thirty-second messages were also part of the audio promotion.

Between 2001 and January 2016, I created twenty-seven 'live' special Powerhouse Radio programs. These one-or-two-hour prerecorded shows were 'real radio,' as I included spoken anecdotes over the track intros every three or four songs. In these programs, we dug deeper into popular artist catalogs without getting too obscure. Even a Ruth Brown, Nina Simone, or Etta James track was slipped into these shows. Powerhouse Radio played R&B from Ray Charles in the late 1950s all the way to modern tracks from the 2000s and beyond. A few one-hit wonders shared the audio stage with all of the memorable legacy artists. Doing this kind of mix is easier said than done. Some older tracks were played as few as four times a year. I had a careful structure. Newer material from the 1970s, 1980s, and 1990s received more exposure. Hence our station tagline was created: "The total #1 R&B Experience."

Information about individual songs written on index cards was an old-school method of cataloging a library. I used this system for all of my digitized music. Red dots on a three-inch by four-inch card identified popular upbeat funk tracks. Blue-dot song cards identified medium to up-tempo tunes. Ballad cards did not use a color code. Each music card noted the artist's name, song title, and how the track ended. All recorded songs ended by either fading out, or with an abrupt 'cold' stop. I did not write down the intro time measured in seconds from the first musical note to the artist's first words. I wasn't talking over records during automation periods. However, songs that began instantly with an immediate artist vocal were identified as having a :00 intro time on index cards.

At times I could have gone live to the world, switching back and forth between automation, but it made more sense to record the programs with dialog in advance. Too much could go wrong during a live show using this untested digital technology. I knew how to do a live program from my professional radio days and didn't need the thrill of 'going live.' A prerecorded program done just like it was live meant better quality control. Because of my experience, I never had to edit them. I used the following steps.

1) In the home studio record on DAT (digital audio tape)
2) Transfer the DAT recoding to PC in wav, then convert to MP3
3) Upload to the Live365 server
4) Schedule the program for playback using the automation system.

Using thousands of index cards made it easy to map out a thirty-hour playlist. The cards could be placed on a very large table or on the floor. A slower alternative without pre-planning was to turn on the computer, log into my Live365 digital music locker, and drag and drop individual song files onto an instantly created playlist. All of my tracks were archived in the music locker. This playlist creation method was inefficient. Only small portions of the playlist could be seen on a laptop screen at a time. The index card method was much better. Twelve to fourteen songs would fill sixty minutes. Three hundred sixty-plus cards identifying music, jingles, and promos (for a thirty-hour playlist) would be manually laid out in order on the floor. When the song sequence was complete, the cards had to be stacked on top of each other. The last card was at the bottom. The remaining cards were stacked in reverse order. When the process was finished, the first song card appeared at the top of the pile. You try it using a dozen sticky notes to better understand the procedure! Finally, I'd just log in to the Live365 automation system and follow the card order to drag and drop the actual song files from the music locker into the digital playlist creation tool. Easy!

Leading into every Christmas, approximately seven days of all classic soul and contemporary jazz holiday music would be played. Every music programmer's December holiday nightmare is how to rotate the two dozen or so popular Christmas melodies without driving people crazy. When the number of Powerhouse Radio Christmas tracks became unwieldy, I experimented one year with Station Playlist Creator. This Windows-based software automation tool created an acceptable blend of tracks in unlimited playlists. The music programmer (me) would stipulate song criteria to guide the software's artificial intelligence. Station Playlist Creator was good, but not good enough to replace the creative human mind. The playlist creator experiment was shut down after one year. Using holiday music index cards was a better system.

Special weekends are a staple of radio. We did our share. I recall several 'one by two' and 'two by one' promotions. How does this work? You play the same song performed by two different artists back-to-back, or you play two different songs by the same artist back-to-back. Some presenters call this promotion 'Two for Tuesday.' I would stage my concept of this soaring song spectacular Friday afternoon through Sunday. We didn't cheat our fans. 'One by two' or 'two by one' is exactly what listeners heard all weekend long, nonstop, with no time-outs.

My favorite weekend special creation was 'Motown from A to Z,' playing all of the Motor City hits from the five main Motown record labels consecutively in order of song title.

Programming this mix required lots of planning! The Digital Millennium Copyright Act of 1998 shackled online broadcasters with prohibitive music rules and high music royalty rates.[29] Music royalties were paid by Live365 for stations with ads. My station, which would become commercial-free after a couple of ad-sponsored years had to pay music royalties and report accurate music usage to licensing companies: ASCAP, BMI, and SESAC. Some of this cost was offset by Powerhouse Radio website advertising and Live365 listeners, who paid a monthly subscription fee to access all stations, whether they were commercial-free or not.

The DMCA prohibits no more than three different songs from the same album within a three-hour period.[30] You couldn't play any more than two of these songs in a row.

In a three-hour period, up to four different songs by the same artist or from the same compilation could be played. No more than three songs from the same artist or compilation could be played back-to-back within this three-hour time frame. AM-FM radio did not have to follow DMCA limitations.

Despite the DMCA chokehold, thousands of broadcasters operated Live365 stations from all over the world. Here's a snapshot of early Powerhouse Radio listener statistics from July 2002 based on hours listened within the month.

Most popular by country:

1) United States

2) United Kingdom

3) Japan

4) Canada

5) France

6) Austria

7) Germany

8)   Australia

9)   South Africa

10)   Republic of Korea

Most popular by USA location:

1)   Washington, DC

2)   Atlanta, GA

3)   Dallas–Fort Worth, TX

4)   New York, New York

5)   Minneapolis–Saint Paul, MN

6)   Los Angeles, CA

7)   Denver, CO

8)   Austin, TX

9)   San Francisco–Oakland, CA

10)   Raleigh–Durham, NC

It was inspiring to receive appreciative feedback from fans and artists. In 2015, I developed a web browser mobile app for Windows with a listen feature and shout-out song box that followers could download for free. Requests, comments, and suggestions would flood into the app.

"This station keeps me Jammin! at work. I can't come into my office without Powerhouse radio. My day is not the same. Thanks for such a powerhouse radio station."

—ART

The app was a great feedback loop for fans. Comments to Powerhouse Radio blog posts extended this connection. Whitney Houston drew the most blog post comments. You may remember the nonstop coverage she received in the tabloids. The year 2001 was hellacious for her in the 'rag mags.' In 2006, I wrote the blog post "The Truth about Whitney Houston," and reader 'browneyez_jr' offered:

> *"I love Whitney Houston and I commend her on the hard work she had put in over the years. I must say that her vocal talent has inspired me, to say the least, as a young gospel artist here on the island of Barbados.*
>
> *What Whitney is going through is hard and as with everyone else facing similar predicaments, she needs the support of those around her. We must not use this time as an opportunity to pull her down just to sell magazines.*
>
> *We must remember that being a celebrity does not make you any less prone to being human. People fall and they get back up."*

You have to keep things interesting for your listeners. When Patti LaBelle and Isaac Hayes offered printed cookbooks, Powerhouse Radio was on it with a "Tasty Tunes with Heart & Soul" contest prize package offering both books together.

The record companies supported us by providing promotional copies of new releases. We'd get either CDs or digital downloads. By requesting duplicate CD copies for special promotions, we'd run contests and give CDs away to our listeners.

"100 Dynamic Duets" was a Valentine's Day special we did based on fan votes off of a special list of songs on our website. The songs were streamed from number 100 to number 1 on Valentine's Day 2005.

Early on, for a short two-year period, "Fab Four Soul" was developed and streamed as a second sister station. Four hundred tracks by jazz and rhythm and blues artists comprised an all-Beatles 24×7 cover song soiree.

Fab Four Soul won a best of Live365 station award. Four hundred tracks were not enough to sustain Fab Four Soul in the long run, so I decided to shut it down and focus on Powerhouse Radio. Looking back, I understand this was the right decision.

Using a dial-up modem to listen to streaming music on a laptop was almost impossible. You were guaranteed disastrous results. In the early days, streaming (on the end-user side) was not very reliable. An improvement was a digital subscriber line. A DSL connection uses the telephone company's copper wiring as a way to minimize streaming dropouts and audio pauses. The technology sped up the delivery speed of the stream. To hear digital music from a faraway city, a laptop or desktop computer was ideal. Mobile listening devices came later.

At its best, DSL was acceptable. At its worst, DSL was awful. The phone company promised a certain transmission speed that was required to listen to uninterrupted music. Sadly, based on my experience, these telecom titans never lived up to their pledge of reliable high-speed service. When the connection would break, sometimes for hours, the phone company repeatedly blamed squirrels. These gnawing critters were accused of snacking on wires in telephone network control boxes. It didn't matter if the box was at the top of a utility pole or on the ground. This blame game happened often.

When I booted DSL and switched to cable internet (four years into Powerhouse Radio), there was a good improvement in listening reliability, but buffering problems persisted. Buffering stops the music stream on the listening device for a second or more as the internet connection tries to keep up with the source feed from the server. Buffering is beyond our control. You might be in Charlotte, NC, while the server is in San Francisco, CA. The flow of digital information must be continuous to avoid hearing audio hiccups. Powerhouse Radio's music was streaming from Live365 servers and not from my home computers. Remember that the Powerhouse Radio song collection was uploaded to Live365 servers and archived there.

I love this technology, but I wouldn't bet my life on it. Digital 4G and 5G mobile speeds help, but there will always be connection outages. Live365 finally created a mobile app for iPhone in 2009 and for Android in 2011. Listening with the Android version was similar to my desktop and laptop computer experiences. Periodic buffering problems happened.

By the end of the sixteen-year Powerhouse Radio run, we had just shy of four thousand digitized tracks for listeners to enjoy. I would say my soulful approach to programming music was more "urban" progressive than southern "neck bone." Whether serving up "Stoned Soul Picnic" by The 5th Dimension or "Fire" by Jimi Hendrix, these morsels of mouth-watering melodies were yummy delights. The key was to place them correctly within song sets. We highlighted some blues tracks too (B.B. King, Albert King) and jazz jams (Les McCann, Grover Washington Jr.). I enjoyed playing them all. The listeners loved the mix.

SATELLITE RADIO AND NPR, WASHINGTON, DC

N PR is an independent nonprofit media organization, also known as National Public Radio, with headquarters in Washington, DC. Over one thousand radio stations partner with NPR in a two-way exchange, feeding the network local stories. These member stations are not called 'affiliates.'

> "*NPR Member Stations are independent, locally owned and oper-ated broadcasters. About two-thirds of stations are licensed to, or are affiliated with, colleges or universities. The remaining third are governed by community-based boards. Some stations are operated jointly with public TV stations. Each Member Station determines its own format and schedule.*"[31]

NPR uses local journalism to strengthen its national and international news. Network correspondents across states and around the globe contrib-ute reports from local international bureaus. Reports from domestic and international sources make their way back to US-based NPR member stations. You'll hear the audio storytelling within NPR News programs as broadcast on local stations. This journalism is also curated for online digital media presentations.

Here's how I joined the network: The NPR hiring experience was quick. Human Resources received my application letter and credentials on December 3, 1999. I interviewed quickly in Washington, DC, on December 13. NPR offered me the job of program manager on December 23.

I tendered my resignation from WHYY effective January 28, 2000. The end of the first month of the new millennium was my last day on the job in Philly.

CD Radio was the original name for NPR's satellite radio division, for which I was hired. Early in 2000, we dumped the anachronistic CD Radio name for the cooler NPR2 sobriquet. This would be the nameplate that represented our branch. Vice President of our sector, Margaret Low, managed the operation. Two program directors were hired. Looking back, staffing had an abundance of riches. Program Director Andrew Morrell led *NPR Talk*. My charge was to pilot *NPR Now*. As you might guess, the *NPR Talk* channel focused on conversation. This was the place to hear live call-in talk shows from member stations.

NPR Now's lineup was more eclectic, offering a wider variety of programs, with two missing features. You would hear NPR-produced programs, independently produced shows, and member station contributions during the 24×7 schedule. Why was it done this way? What you did not hear was *Morning Edition* or *All Things Considered*. These were and remain the two most popular NPR news programs.

Margaret Low organized a station-based advisory group of managers who encouraged us not to place those two NPR News magazines on satellite radio. Simple economics was at the core of the managers' argument. Local fundraising would suffer if listeners could bypass local on-air station appeals by tuning into a satellite radio feed without hearing fundraising. They did not want the two NPR flagship programs to be part of the service. NPR could not fundraise on the subscription-based satellite radio service. Here's the fear: Some listeners might turn off the local *Morning Edition* broadcast and switch over to satellite radio to hear the same program if their station was fundraising during *Morning Edition*. Local station managers were not buying the prose from the NPR on Sirius mission statement that promised, "The advent of satellite radio does NOT mean that everyone's piece of the pie will shrink. Rather, it means that we are baking a bigger pie." The mission statement also drew attention to a prediction by some that "early adapters to satellite radio will be younger than public radio's core audience. This is an important demographic for us to reach."

According to The Corporation for Public Broadcasting, "the median age of public media listeners has roughly tracked the median age of baby boomers."

After brainstorming with the local station managers, NPR senior leadership agreed that there would be no *Morning Edition* or *All Things Considered* on *NPR Now* or *NPR Talk*.

How would you go after more news-consuming thirty-four to fifty-five-year-olds? Perhaps you'd use a more contemporary approach and develop an NPR News program still based on high journalism standards but mixed with a touch of twenty-first-century informality. We tried to create that program two different times.

You are not relevant on morning radio without a compelling morning program. *The Way In* was piloted as a wake-up news program for *NPR Now* to fulfill this need.

I hinted at "the abundance of riches" for the *CD Radio* staff. Here it is in November 2000. The order of names reflects our position in a montage of photos featured in the *@NPR* newsletter. In September 2000, the job title of Program Manager was reclassified to Program Director. Here's the NPR2 team:

Hannah Misol, Production Assistant	*The Way In*
Susan Stone, Producer	*Take Notes*
Kathryn Simmons, Associate Producer	*NPR Talk*
Melinda Wittsock, Host	*The Way In*
Carline Windall Watson, Associate Producer / Director	*The Way In*
Leah Fleming, Production Assistant	*The Way In*
Laurie Howell, Announcer	*NPR Talk*
Margaret Low, Vice President	*NPR2*
David Srebnik, Associate Producer	*NPR Now*
Kingsley H. Smith, Program Director	*NPR Now*
Andrew Morrell, Program Director	*NPR Talk*
John Buckley, Editor	*The Way In*
Nancy Marshall-Genzer, Announcer	*NPR Now*
J.J. Sutherland, Senior Producer	*The Way In*
Joyce Stuber, Traffic Manager	*NPR 2*
Suzanne Mesnick, Technical Director	*NPR2*
Gay Williams, Budget Manager	*NPR2*

You might find a similar delegation of duties at a local radio station. The structure seemed reasonable. What we didn't know later on would hurt our strategy to develop both *NPR2* channels.

We expected Sirius Satellite Radio to be the first US company to beam programs down from the ionosphere to car-based receivers. NPR's satellite distribution agreement was with Sirius Satellite Radio. Our expectation was that we'd be operational early in 2000. This didn't happen.

Delays are always expected with the deployment of technology. A two-year delay for us (on the Sirius Satellite Radio side) was devastating. XM Satellite Radio beat Sirius as the first cosmic service provider. XM hit the go button in September 2001. Both NPR2 channels finally launched on Valentine's Day, 2002, using the AudioVault automation system. July 2002 is noted as the official Sirius Satellite Radio launch.

Sadly, NPR could not sustain the level of personnel needed to support NPR2 during the two-year wait. *The Way In* and most of its staff were the victims of 2001 budget cuts. In June 2001, I left *NPR Now* to join NPR's online division to produce live web events with PBS. The Public Broadcasting Service distributes programs to public television stations.

During the long wait for Sirius Satellite Radio sign-on, I attended a presentation given by competitor XM's programming leader, Lee Abrams. He may or may not have known that I was seated at his gathering. Abrams is famous in the radio industry for his use of research to build audiences. He and his partner, Kent Burkhart, created a successful consulting business in the 1980s. During the Abrams presentation, he offered this prediction for the future: "News programming will be the new Top 40." I never forgot that quote. To some extent, he was right. Today, three major cable news channels are testaments to his prophecy.

So what else did NPR on Satellite Radio do for the presentation of morning information? Our second wake-up news magazine, *The Bryant Park Project*, did see the light of day, airing Monday to Friday from 7:00 a.m. to 9:00 a.m. (EST). *The Bryant Park Project* survived for just two years (2007-2008). The 2008 housing crisis crashed the stock market, challenged employers, and jettisoned employees. At NPR, many *BPP* folks felt the impact. Their show had to go due to cost cutting.

● ● ● ● ●

Before timely news magazines could be presented in the morning, we aired rollover programs from the previous day, including *Fresh Air* with Terry Gross. Multiple replays padded out the morning schedule.

Another original program launched in 2006 on the NPR Now satellite channel was *From Scratch*, created by independent producer Jessica Harris. I helped Jessica guide *From Scratch* to maturity over the next several years.

The theme of the program was similar to that of another one in my past. At WHYY FM in Philadelphia, I worked with an independent producer, Rutgers University Professor Dr. Kim Ezra Shienbaum. She used our studio facilities. Kim developed an entrepreneurial capitalism radio series called *Success Stories*, where she interviewed CEOs. *Success Stories* did not air on WHYY FM.

On SiriusXM, *From Scratch* with Jessica Harris would follow a similar *Success Stories* theme. The NPR network would also roll out its own iteration of a true founder's 'rags to riches' tale with another talk show, *How I Built This*, featuring host Guy Raz. This conversation exposé was developed by NPR's Vice President of Programming, Eric Nuzum, in 2016. More on Guy Raz in another chapter.

In July 2008, the FCC approved a satellite radio union between operators Sirius and XM. The merged company is now SiriusXM.

As reported by *Barron's*, 32.4 million paid subscribers used the SiriusXM service in the first quarter of 2023.[32] The investor section of the SiriusXM website reported that 23.9 million subscribers closed out

2012 for the satellite broadcaster.[33] *The Infinite Dial*, a yearly investigative "survey of digital media consumer behavior in America" by *Edison Research*, revealed in their twenty-fifth anniversary summary (2023) that Satellite Radio listening is way below AM and FM, owned digital music, podcasts, online audio and CD player sampling in the car.[34] Their survey was based on "audio sources currently ever used in a car (US age eighteen-plus and has driven/ridden in a car in the last month; 87 percent)."

Two decades of very weak growth suggest that Satellite Radio might have been and still could be a safe home for sharing the wealth of NPR's in-depth news magazines.

There's more to my NPR story. By 2013, I was programming three NPR channels for SiriusXM: two for broadcast and one for online only. NPR moved into a brand-new state-of-the-art broadcast center in DC. When one of my NPR coworkers left the company, another opportunity presented itself with international implications.

NPR BERLIN, GERMANY

What were my chances of being invited to two different receptions in Berlin, Germany, by ambassadors of the United States of America?

First, let's roll back the clock to 2006. On March 8, 2006, the Media Authority of Berlin-Brandenburg (MABB) issued a license authorizing NPR to broadcast on FM frequency 104.1 from April 1, 2006, through March 31, 2013.

The license was issued to NPR Media Berlin GGMBH, a German nonprofit entity and wholly owned subsidiary of NPR. NPR Media Berlin GGMBH began broadcasting on April 1, 2006.

We looked to English-speaking Germans as well as English speakers living in Berlin to listen to and support 104.1 FM.

Much of the credit for this collaboration goes to Jeff Rosenberg, the director of NPR Worldwide. Residents in European, Mideast and Asian countries could receive NPR programs using NPR Worldwide's direct-to-home satellite technology, radio station rebroadcasts, and cable system transmissions.

Using this approach, NPR Worldwide reached the majority of English speakers around the globe.

NPR Worldwide Director Jeff Rosenberg worked during the early 2000s on the acquisition of the Berlin FM frequency 104.1.

FM licensing authority for the frequency switched often after World War II. Voice of America was the last entity to control the Berlin frequency before NPR was able to win approval for the channel from the MABB. NPR Berlin was the only radio station ever licensed to NPR.

In 1942, the state-owned Voice of America began radio transmissions around the world to counterbalance Nazi propaganda.[35]

According to its charter, VOA:

> *"serves as a consistently reliable and authoritative source of news, presents a balanced and comprehensive projection of significant American thought and institutions; presents the policies of the United States clearly and effectively, as well as discussions and opinion on these policies."*[36]

In late 2007, Jeff Rosenberg retired. I was enthusiastic about the opportunity offered to me to assume responsibility for the daily operation of NPR International Services (Worldwide) and NPR Berlin. Three SiriusXM channels also remained under my programming umbrella.

We had non-NPR freelance journalists covering different news, information, and entertainment beats in Berlin. Before the Zoom video collaboration tool, three-minute audio reports were filed primarily by lead journalist Monika Mueller-Kroll using various digital distribution methods from Germany to NPR headquarters in Washington, DC.

Life In Berlin features were the core of these three-minute summaries focusing on arts and culture.

There was no studio facility in Berlin. We did record weather reports from DC. We operated the FM Berlin website from DC. Three-minute local Berlin audio reports were played adjacent to NPR News at the two-minute cutaway point.

NPR provides live newscasts out of Washington, DC, and Culver City, California. Five-minute top-of-the-hour newscasts begin at one minute past. At two minutes in, local stations can cover the last three minutes of the network newscast with their own local content.

During my seventeen and a half years at NPR, two different radio automation systems (AudioVault and David) were used to send the magic to NPR Worldwide and NPR Berlin. Our NPR automation systems pushed the digital digits to the SiriusXM automation system for transmission of our three channels.

Ambassador Philip D. Murphy (who later became Governor of New Jersey) honored NPR President and CEO Vivian Schiller and NPR Berlin staff with a reception at the ambassador's German residence in 2010.

On Schiller's way to the reception, a language problem caused some static. Everyone in Berlin speaks English. Well, almost everyone. Before the ride-sharing service Uber took over (Uber's 2011 European debut was in Paris), what could you do when your cab driver didn't speak that much English? You could reach out to a translator. NPR Berlin Production Assistant Sara Richards rose to the occasion to straighten out the driving logistics while on the mobile phone with the cabbie. CEO Vivian arrived safely.

I returned to Berlin in 2014. Ambassador to the United States John B. Emerson invited Berlin-based and stateside NPR folks to a reception at the Ambassador's residence in Berlin. On both trips (2010 and 2014), community meet-and-greet events were held to rub elbows with NPR Berlin fans in the city.

A highlight was a May 24, 2014, event at Sophiensaele in Mitte Berlin, hosted by NPR's Guy Raz, that was recorded and broadcast on 104.1 FM in June.

Fundraising periods were added to NPR Berlin by 2014, since it was a noncommercial public radio station in Germany. Using the DC automation system, live appeals for financial support from our people in both Berlin and DC were launched for the radio and online audience.

When the time zone difference is six hours, nothing beat coming into NPR Washington, DC, facilities at midnight (EST) to do live 6:00 a.m. Berlin fundraising. We electronically connected the 104.1 team in Berlin to participate live with us in DC. Hats off to our DC-based interns who helped support decorum in the studio.

● ● ● ● ●

TO BE OR NOT TO BE AN INTERN

I was never an intern. Luckily college radio was good enough for me to land first jobs at two different places: WRVR as a mixing control board operator and WALL as an announcer.

When an NPR intern fulfills future goals by earning external professional opportunities, they continue the cycle of assimilating and transferring knowledge.

Here's what one NPR Berlin intern remembers:

"My experience as an intern at NPR was truly invaluable. The work helped reassure me that I'd chosen the right career path, as I

came to the office every day so excited to absorb as much as I could from veterans in the building like Kingsley. I was constantly blown away by the talent and creativity inside NPR HQ — and amazed by the generosity of the pros to help me develop new skills.

"The internship also helped me secure full-time employment as a public radio reporter, after freelancing for a couple of years. I've remained in public radio for nearly a decade since my NPR internship in winter 2014, and I've enjoyed every minute of it. I've also been lucky enough to work with and mentor several talented young journalists who've interned with us at VPM News, including one who is now a full-time producer at NPR.

"I'm so proud to be part of the public radio family, and I truly hope NPR will continue its internship program for generations to come."

—MEGAN PAULY, JANUARY 2014 NPR BERLIN INTERN

VPM News is a part of Virginia Public Media. I salute Megan and the entire family of NPR interns, who performed fantastic work in every division of the company!

• • • • •

You'll get euros and dollars from donors everywhere during simultaneous on-air and online fundraising. Such was the case during NPR Berlin's 10th anniversary fundraising pledge drive in 2016. This was our last fundraiser. We did meet our goal.

NPR FM Berlin was able to acquire Berlin-based studio space for the first time in 2016. It was a brand-new studio facility too!

Later that year, when the vice president of my division called me into her Washington, DC office to say that she'd been charged with reducing $100,000 from her budget, I knew some hard decisions lay ahead for me and her.

NPR investigated transferring the Berlin license in late 2016 to a local group, Friends of NPR Berlin, represented by Karen Roth, Susan Woosley, Heidy Kwan, Svetlana Stepanova, and John C. Kornblum, former Assistant US Secretary of State for European Affairs and former deputy US Ambassador to NATO.

John and Karen were influential in drawing attention to the NPR Berlin license goal granted by MABB in 2006 and renewed in 2013.

By 2017, it was eventually decided, with Kornblum's encouragement, that California public radio station KCRW would assume operation of NPR Berlin. Now a nine-hour time difference loomed large between Santa Monica and Berlin.

Under the leadership of KCRW President Jennifer Ferro, the partnership lasted only until December 2020. Financial pressure, along with the pandemic, closed the door on this cultural experiment.[37]

In chapter seven (WHYY), I mentioned my first exposure as an employee to the pressure to raise dollars faced by public media companies. This cycle tends to reappear every decade. In 1983, it was the nationwide 'Drive to Survive' fundraising campaign. Ten years later, in the mid-1990s, Newt Gingrich led the charge to defund public broadcasting. In 2008, it was the nationwide economic contraction caused by the housing market crash that affected everyone, including NPR. The nonprofit news network was forced to make numerous tweaks from 2010 to 2020 to nurture balanced budgets. Jump to March 2023, when NPR lays off 10 percent of its 1,100 workforce, hoping to level off with 990 employees.

The list of NPR CEOs has been long since 1983. All these leaders have verbalized the same goal as a tonic for growth. Get a younger audience. Get a more diverse audience.

Expansion attempts have not produced consistent results. New hosts and their programs come and go for different reasons. Skilled industry pros Derek McGinty, Tavis Smiley, Ed Gordon, Juan Williams, Joshua Johnson, and others have all passed through the NPR pipeline.

Why haven't NPR's expansion tactics and strategies worked? NPR bylaws limit total autonomy for member station partnerships. This might squander some big-thinking NPR ideas that are generated internally. Then there are rules governing what qualifies a public media outlet as a CPB-funded entity. There are restrictions. You'll read more about financial governance in a later chapter. The bottom line: lack of money prevents an explosion of impactful innovation to serve those targeted communities that would expand the listening audience. Could more popular culture narratives bring in more listeners? This approach is controversial. Appealing to the less educated with trendy topics is viewed by some as dumbing down the enterprise. Research does tell us that highly educated folks flock to public radio and television. Still, the reader class represents only a slice of the *Morning Edition* or *PBS NewsHour* audience.

These are some of the factors involved in explaining why nothing has really changed in the public media funding model for the last fifty years. Noncommercial community service to America through news and entertainment is why these media pillars need to survive.

A combination of user donations, subscriptions, digital pay walls, and corporate donor support may be the future salvation of the public media enterprise. The small percentage of government funding stations receive may dry up.

● ● ● ● ●

I enjoyed my long tenure with NPR, working out of their flagship head-quarters in Washington, DC. Under no pressure to leave, I decided to tender my resignation to my boss, Anya Grundmann, Senior Vice President for programming and audience development. I gave her six weeks' notice, providing ample time for a decision on a replacement plan. I left in July 2017 with the prospect of just vacationing for six months. My NPR position was not replaced. Essentially, my move was semi-retirement after forty-five and a half years as a broadcast professional. From a miserly $6,760 per year full-time radio salary in 1975 to a fortunate six-figure salary in 2017, yes, it was all worth it. In January 2018, I turned a hobby into a second calling by ramping up my software application development skills to go full speed ahead with my twenty-first-century business.

Before I briefly touch upon that calling, you must hear about how I explored cities of fame from coast to coast.

BATTLE OF THE RADIO CONFERENCES

I've attended five industry-specific conventions, some of them multiple times:

Black Radio Exclusive (BRE)
Public Radio Conference (PRC)
Public Radio Program Directors Conference (PRPD)
Development Exchange, Inc. (DEI) / Greater Public
Live365 Conference in San Francisco

Many regional conferences also power local grassroots movements across the USA. Three other media jamborees should be mentioned. First, "Jack the Rapper." Second, NABJ (National Association of Black Journalists). Third, the one-hundred-year-old giant of broadcast gatherings, the NAB. It was founded in 1923 as the National Association of Radio Broadcasters until television was subsumed into the name in 1951. The National Association of Radio and Television Broadcasters became the NAB in 1958. I haven't attended the NAB conference, NABJ, or Jack the Rapper.

Who was Jack the Rapper, the person, and what was Jack the Rapper, the convention? Joseph Gibson Jr. a.k.a. 'Jockey Jack' (1922–2000), was a famous Black deejay who created a showcase for Black music, radio, and kindred personalities by throwing his 'party' conference. Jack's convention reflected his name and the aura of his pulsating on-air vocal style. He was inducted into the Black Radio Hall of Fame in 1989.

NABJ was founded in Washington, DC, in 1975. Clinton C. Wilson, in his book *Whither the Black Press? Glorious Past, Uncertain Future* says:

> *"A critical mass of Black journalists working in White-owned general audience media had become large enough to form a national organization. More important, the exodus of journalists from the Black press to the White daily media that began during the urban riots of the mid-1960s was bifurcating the African American marketplace for news."*[38]

Wilson elaborates on the tensions between NABJ's mission statement and 1975 reality. The ambitious Black talent pool was splitting into two branches. One group worked in Black media; the other group embraced general market opportunities. I understand the pressure. NABJ is a fascinating story. You might want to learn more about it.

Regardless of the conference name, networking opportunities are a big draw. Learning experiences are everywhere. Informal socializing rules the moment. Free or paid, promotional swag sits waiting to be swiped by human fingers faster than an eagle snatches a field mouse.

Conferences are cool for fun, but they can also be catalysts for career growth. Money, logistics, and travel might stand in the way of broadcast personnel if expenses are not paid for by the employer. Budget means you may not be able to go if you are not part of the management team.

Since I wasn't in that supervisory circle by mid-1981, it was worth it to bolt down to Houston, Texas, using some saved funds for the *Black Radio Exclusive* convention.

Black Radio Exclusive (*BRE*) was an early Black music trade magazine founded by the late Sidney Miller in 1976. My article "What It Means to Be a Progressive Black Radio Station" was published that year in *BRE*.

My best memory from the 1981 *BRE* Conference swinging soiree was Cheryl Lynn capturing the moment performing "Shake It Up Tonight," her hit song produced and arranged by Ray Parker Jr.

Later in August 1981, MTV Music Television would roll out its non-stop buffet of one-dimensional pop videos. By 1983, Michael Jackson's popularity had forced more variety into the channel.

Stateside conferences are a great way to see America. You feel like an NFL, NBA, or MLB athlete jetting to Boston, Miami, Memphis, Minneapolis, Phoenix, Seattle, or San Diego. Travel is always based on the convention destination in a given year.

On the PRC and PRPD public radio conference playing field, people score points for hosting skill-building seminars. In 2004, in San Antonio, Texas, I moderated "Basics: An Introduction to Core Values" with a panel of news directors and program directors (at the PRPD summit).

The chapter on WHYY briefly touches on core values. These standards, introduced in a PRPD 2000 research project, used eloquent prose primarily vocalized by listeners to explain why public radio programming had appeal.[39]

PRPD printed these distilled listener observations on double-sided three-inch by four-inch cards. The language was concise.

If you had space in your wallet or purse, you could stuff all three cards inside. Here is the trio, with their categories representing listener observations. It's a blueprint of commandments.

1)	Public Radio's Core Values
2)	Jazz Core Values
3)	Classical Core Values

Each card had three sections: **Qualities of the Mind, Qualities of the Heart and Spirit,** and **Qualities of Craft.** The three top-line categories are broken down further with slight changes according to genre.

The universal Qualities of the Mind include "Lifelong Learning, Substance, Curiosity, Credibility, Accuracy, Honesty, Respect for Listeners, and Purpose."

Classical Qualities of the Heart and Spirit boast subjective "Peaceful, Soothing, and Relaxing" words to heed.

Universal **Qualities of Craft** stress "a uniquely human voice, Conversational, Authentic, intimate Pacing, Attention to detail—music, sound elements, language."

There's much more, but let's close with what's imprinted on the front of the "Public Radio's Core Values" card. "It is the fusion, the crosscutting, of these three sets of qualities (Mind, Heart, and Spirit) that have created public radio's signature sound."[40]

The trio of two-sided cheat sheets, slightly bigger than a standard business card, spelled out everything in context.

● ● ● ● ●

You'd find lots of radio programmers at the annual PRPD summit. The PRC (Public Radio Conference) assembled a larger universe of noncommercial stakeholders who thought about "big picture ideas."

- What was the role of new technology?
- How can we grow our audience?
- Do public radio newsrooms and staff reflect the demographic mix of America?
- Are we training the next generation of talent?
- How can we raise more money with effective fundraising and broader outreach?

At the PRC, new programs were launched. Focus groups were held. Large seminars informed. Big social functions added a larger group dimension to private one-on-one meetings.

My one Development Exchange, Inc. (DEI)/Greater Public conference was in New York City. DEI was all about fundraising, corporate sponsorship opportunities, and expanding financial growth.

Live365's 2004 Broadcaster Summit in San Francisco, CA, had a familiar conference schedule. Online-streaming disciples attended from all over the world. A long weekend meant meet-and-greets, dining with new friends, and parties.

You bet there was lots of serious discussion at the summit. Here are a few of the actual sessions:

- "Licensing and Royalty Issues"
- "The Future of the Internet Radio Industry"

- "Indie Music in the Age of Media Monopolies"
- "Making Money with Internet Radio"
- "Attracting (and Retaining) More Listeners"

Betty Ray, Live 365 Senior Editor and Director of Community, assisted in organizing this summit. Trivia note: Betty helped build the webcasting initiative for Garrison Keillor's "A Prairie Home Companion." She is an alum of Minnesota Public Radio.

•   •   •   •   •

I must acknowledge what happened one year during the conference cavalcade of rotating cities. My convention destination was only thirty-five miles from Washington, DC. It was the first time this organization held court in this charming city. Who wouldn't want to connect with colleagues while eyeing a historic view of the rejuvenated Baltimore Inner Harbor?

Sadly, event plans came to a screeching halt. The expected PRPD gathering faced a costly decision. PRPD Executive Director Marcia Alvar stated in *Current*, a news periodical for public media, that "no one wanted to leave home."[41]

PRPD's conference was promoted months in advance. Now it was derailed and had to be cancelled. The first day of activity would have been September 12, 2001, the day after the terrorist attacks.

•   •   •   •   •

Conferences are important. I've attended others that are outside the scope of this Powerhouse Radio story: four Comic Cons, two *Ancient Aliens* encounters, two Consumer Electronic Shows (CES), and one Game Devs of Color Expo.

Let's return to my story as I un-bottle a reservoir of radio reflections and share a handful of musical moments.

NEW HORIZONS AND RADIO TODAY

How did I turn a twenty-three-year part-time hobby into a full-time second career? Before my closing thoughts about radio, here's a very brief summary of my full-time dive into tech. A full-time effort came together slowly in January 2018.

I had previous teaching experience. My students tackled website design at a Southern New Jersey computer school in the 1990s. During the same period, I also taught computer basics to teachers at a middle school in Philadelphia.

That background reflected a multiple-job persona. I always had two or three gigs going at the same time, even if some were part-time opportunities.

My first mobile phone-based app in 2012 was a modest hit. I was a part-time business hobbyist in the software world. Would this prove to be unfortunate serendipity for a very inexperienced mobile developer?

I had solid knowledge as a desktop developer using Visual Basic and Windows software to create the Empower Encyclopedia CD-ROM, an early Black History project. The Empower Encyclopedia took five years to research and complete during the pre-online explosion days of the early 1990s. It was finally released to the marketplace in the summer of 1998.

What about that first mobile app? Rhythm music games were all the rage by 2012. I dropped Hip Hop Fingers into the Google Play market as the first mobile game app released under the Quikthinking Software moniker. That's my business certificate of trade name, registered in 1989, the year after I graduated from Rutgers University.

As a radio lifer who played music on-air as well as talked and wrote about it professionally, I felt it made sense to pursue this game idea as the first offering to the growing mobile app universe.

Before pulling Hip Hop Fingers out of Google Play, this music rhythm game had been downloaded organically well over fifty thousand times. No paid advertising was used. A music rhythm game is played while listening to tracks while the player taps correctly to the beat on synced music notes falling from the top of the user's screen. I selected eighteen royalty-free tracks. What was the price of development? My time and opportunity cost to learn Google's operating system, Android. The app was also distributed in other Android app stores, but the download tally in *Google Play* was the one I paid attention to.

Although the first app did very well for a first-timer, acquiring more skills to advance and compete was a rough road. As Powerhouse Radio is the focus of what you've read up to this point, I'll quickly wrap up the summary about the late dawn of my second career.

Between 2017 and 2022, my level of mobile app development expertise required growth. I had to make a quantum leap from inexperience to intermediate. I did that. Next, to master the advanced Android and iOS dance of development, I had to take advanced training to tango with difficult code. It was a must to reach this high level, dominated by experts. Today, I don't call myself a fancy dancer pirouetting with screens full of code. I'm not an expert yet, but I can cruise comfortably in this space as long as I continue to adapt to the changes and learn more.

• • • • •

THE POWER IN THE POWERHOUSE

Everyone wants to have influence. Every radio station or network wants to be a powerhouse. The term "powerhouse" is bestowed on the best influential achievers. Few reach the mark. The main title of this book was inspired by the powerhouse phrase and its role as the identifier of my deceased online radio stream.

DIRTY DEEDS AND RISKY BUSINESS

What common threads of talent pool conduct have I witnessed? Think about the comedic hijinks that pepper the smorgasbord of wacky behavior. College radio pranks are innocent:

- Lighting a colleague's news copy on fire while they are reading it live.

- Killing the lights in a studio or scrambling (unplugging) portions of a control board before your relief sits down to begin a live shift. We'd do this as a skill test during my college radio days! You had to be very sharp to succeed in this trial by fire.

Some of this silly stuff continues to happen once you reach the pros. If radio is theater of the mind, radio troubadours are operatic thespians of drama, fun, anger, and addictions. I was exposed to a no-holds-barred view of humor-to-carnage activity when I was a rank-and-file performer. Later, my gaze, looking down from my perch as a middle manager at rank-and-file employees, was no different.

I witnessed lots of salacious behavior when I was in the trenches and did not possess a role in management. Imagine a six-pack beer-boozing morning performer falling off their studio chair just two and a half hours into a four-hour shift. Yes, it happened on multiple occasions to the same person. Ponder the weed-wacked overnight automaton medicating their mind to the max with classical grass. Can you believe another paper magazine hound who gazed at their personal bookrack full of hardcore pornography in a radio studio to pass the time? Wasn't this a creepy diversion from their job? I guess this individual's mind was not engaged in their work.

These anecdotes are all true. Frankly, I saw less debauchery when immersed in the music artist community.

You know that performing artists have their pleasures too. I saw one palatial hotel suite laid out with a chemist's brew of pharmaceutical edibles. This left an abstainer like me feeling that I really didn't belong inside this one music person's ad hoc buffet of forbidden consumable treats!

A HARD HABIT TO BREAK

Radio continues to be my number-one media habit. Over a dozen physical units congregate around the square footage of my home. They are plugged in or battery-operated. But that's not all. Two different smart speakers are also used at home to sample broadcast stations from all over the USA. Smart speakers are voice-activated. I've been fortunate to not only use these speakers but also to participate in research studies about them by recording test voice prompts for third parties (not the manufacturers).

Operating a broadcast mixing control board has been mentioned in a few chapters of my story. Human control board operators who ignite the audio levels of microphones and music for a second person (the host) in the broadcast studio have mostly disappeared. Elevators once had human operators too. Combo operations now rule on-air radio workspaces. These are shops where the announcer does double duty, controlling all the technical elements. Only at the largest stations and networks do control board engineers survive. Time marches on. Today's radio automation systems can output music and any other performance element you can imagine. The live announcer only needs to know how to turn on their microphone and talk. Automation can activate the mic if it is programmed to do so.

With a high-speed internet connection from a laptop or mobile phone, anyone can connect remotely to a studio far away. You can do the same thing with your social media account and go live to the world in real time.

HOW IS RADIO DOING?

As far as the state of radio in 2023 is concerned, all is not well. Public Radio continues to run on its cyclical hamster wheel, chasing sustainable funding.

Local public radio and television stations only receive a small fraction of their budgets from the government. The percentage has remained stable since the Public Broadcasting Act of 1967 kick-started the system.

Tim Karr details in *Common Dreams* why the 2022 USA appropriation from Congress of $465 million to the Corporation for Public Broadcasting is minuscule compared to the UK, France, Denmark, Japan, and South Korea. Karr explains this in terms of per capita.[42]

The *World Book Encyclopedia Dictionary* defines per capita as "divided among a number of individuals in equal shares, as an inheritance or estate."[43] Here's how it looks for the example countries, according to Karr:

USA	$1.40 per capita
South Korea	$14
Japan	$53
France	$75
United Kingdom	$81
Denmark	$93
Finland	$100
Norway	$110

Each dollar amount may fluctuate annually. European and Asian countries have alternate ways of funding public radio and television. Citizens may pay a yearly tax that they can't opt out of. Stateside, the Corporation for Public Broadcasting says:

> "Federal funds, distributed through CPB grants to local stations, provide critical seed money and basic operating support. Stations leverage each $1 of federal funding to raise over $6 from other sources — including state and local governments, philanthropic foundations, private businesses, and universities — a tremendous return on the taxpayer investment."[44]

CPB must provide 95 percent of its appropriation as grants to local television and radio stations. What percentage of a local budget is this? A wide range exists depending on the station.

- For the 2021–2022 fiscal year, about 4.97 percent of KUT Austin, Texas, and KUTX's projected revenue came from the CPB. Both are radio properties.[45]
- In 2011, KCRW Santa Monica, CA, General Manager Jennifer Ferro reported that CPB funding amounted to 9 percent of the station's radio operating budget.[46]
- For Maine Public Radio, approximately 11 percent of 2020's operational revenue came from the CPB.[47]
- Total government funding for WHYY FM Philadelphia, PA, radio and television for fiscal year 2022 was 10 percent of revenue.[48]

How much money does a public station raise from listeners or viewers? Every year, the percentage of revenue from dedicated supporters has hovered close to 50 percent. That amount hasn't changed in decades. There are outliers. Arizona PBS television in Phoenix receives up to 80 percent of its revenue from viewers.[49]

While consumers of public broadcasting generally love what they support, commercial radio fans express mixed emotions about what they hear. Music, talk, and commercials reign supreme in this profit-making triumvirate. The ads just keep coming. It's an experience tolerated in exchange for free access to the media. Gone are the days of three-to-four-minute ad breaks.

Unless you are listening to commercial-free Satellite Radio music channels (full disclosure: I've been a subscriber since 2002), you'll be tortured by 10-minute or longer commercial breaks on the AM and FM audio highways.

Advertising competitors are routinely placed back-to-back in the same ad break. You may have seen this on television. Think about the different car manufacturers segmenting back-to-back without separation.

Local radio micro-formatics hygiene is bathing in a body wash of sloppiness. For example, if an event happens two weeks away, you might tease that it's happening on 'Thursday, May 2nd.' To promote it correctly, the day before it happens, you'd say it's happening 'tomorrow,' and on the day of the event, you'd say 'today.' I'm still hearing big city radio events being promoted after the fact by mistake or by neglect. All they have to do is record multiple versions. That's the best way to have a more intimate rapport with the listeners.

Here's another quirk: Do you think I would be justified to precede the next paragraph by saying, "If you're just starting to read this book . . .?" Some radio folks use this tactic all the time: "If you've just tuned in . . .." I never understood why, especially on public radio, hosts do this. All they need to do is reintroduce a guest or subject and move on. Radio is generally not for appointment listening, so people constantly tune in and out. There is no need to apologize to those who are already with you.

• • • • •

DOES ANYBODY REALLY KNOW WHAT TIME IT IS?

Working in radio during the pre-automation days taught local deejays and control board operators how to correctly back-time music. What does this mean? Here's the timing challenge: a newscast or other program element starts at exactly the top of the next hour. Back-timing a song means starting it prior to the close of the current hour, so it ends at the exact start point of the coming top of the hour element. When this is done, the final song or music instrumental closing the old hour does not have to be faded out by the control board operator going into the new hour. How is this done? Consider an example. Start a three-minute, thirty-five-second song or a three minutes and thirty-five-second instrumental at fifty-six minutes twenty-five seconds past the current hour. The music content will end at exactly 00:00 (the top of the next hour). If the song did not start 'live' on air but was started correctly at fifty-six minutes twenty-five seconds, we call this a dead roll. The actual sound of a dead roll joins the live audio chain when automation or an operator raises the volume so you can hear it.

Many audio performers coming from the podcasting world are inexperienced at jumping in and out of live network programs and events. Automation systems have replaced the need for people to develop hands-on time-calculation practices.

Finicky local automation systems may drift by a second with out-of-town network automation systems, so you sometimes hear the sound of two audio sources simultaneously.

Do you like tests? How about those required Federal Communications Commission **Emergency Alert System** tests? EAS tests are required by FCC rules and must follow FCC rule requirements. The FCC says:

> *"The Emergency Alert System (EAS) is a national public warning system that requires broadcasters, cable television systems, wireless cable systems, wireline video providers, satellite digital audio radio service providers and direct broadcast satellite service providers to make their communications facilities available to the President during a National emergency. The system also may be used by state*

and local authorities to deliver important emergency information such as AMBER alerts and severe weather warnings targeted to specific geographical regions or areas."[50]

There are many more technical details that don't need explanation here. Stations must maintain encoders, decoders, and signal-generating EAS equipment. For listeners, these tests now pop into radio broadcasts at any time rather than at a natural programming break. Past practice allowed stations to schedule the EAS test at a specific time. Station broadcast content could also be scheduled around the test (if the test could not be moved) for a better listener experience. Today, the EAS audio test will insert itself anywhere, anytime, just like ads shoehorn their way into a YouTube video.

FCC rules change. Stations must follow Commission updates. EAS test alerts do jar the senses when they appear uninvited. At least you can decide if you want to hear them on your mobile phone!

BRING ON THE NOISE

Much of this book was written from late 2020 to 2023, during the height of the COVID-19 pandemic. Many broadcasters had to become work-at-home computer experts during this crisis. I was lucky that NPR issued every employee in the news division a laptop in 2013, giving us lots of time to become confident in accessing critical work systems remotely. Almost all NPR employees would eventually receive a laptop.

Let's talk about noise. I'm sure you'll agree that the most annoying thing about a video, podcast, television channel, or radio channel is an unsavory variance in the sound level.

For years, most radio signals have used magic boxes to compress audio so stations eliminate overmodulation. These boxes also normalize low levels to a higher output level. You wouldn't know this if you listened to some network and local radio purveyors. What's the takeaway for these institutions? Watch your levels!

There are certain local stations I listen to, and I can tell who is operating the broadcast console during live segments just by hearing the wide variance in sound levels. How do I know? Hosts who have the privilege of working with a separate control board operator frequently give their tech's name an on-air shout-out. I associate their names with their mastery of skills. Within ten minutes of the next opportunity to tune in during the same time period on subsequent days, just by listening, I knew who was there. No need to hear a name shout-out.

Some stations technically turn down maximum compression to keep the broadcast sound as natural as possible. Think of the difference between music on vinyl and music on a compact disc. The digital version is not as warm. Highly compressed stations have a fast whooshing or pumping sound when folks start talking in the clear or over music. It is much easier to hear this on AM radio.

Talk radio suffers from a noticeable mobile phone assault on the ears. The fidelity of a cellphone conversation heard on a broadcast just can't match the better quality of a landline. You can tell when a radio talk show caller is using a landline. Poor mobile phone voice quality is probably here to stay until the technology improves and you can't hear the difference.

Did you know there is a correct sequencing of word order and language required to read a good weather forecast correctly? It's the same with vertical and horizontal promotion of program elements and events. Vertical promotion explains what is coming up next or later the same day in the schedule. Horizontal promotion expresses what is coming up at the same time tomorrow.

It's the program manager's, program director's, or content manager's job to teach these skills to those under their direction. Maybe these supervisory people need to start listening to their own stations with a critical ear. The death of radio has been predicted forever. I don't believe traditional radio will end anytime soon. Radio in the hands of either local or corporate ownership is still an influential community partner and friend for listeners.

A wildcard hostile to the long-term existence of AM radio is the movement to eliminate the broadcast band from new electric vehicles. Manufacturers claim that motors in EVs generate electromagnetic interference, causing AM reception problems. Radio trade groups are trying to rally public support against this trend.

WHAT IT TAKES TO MOVE AHEAD

Traffic scheduling is not the sexiest position at a broadcast facility. Traffic managers and their subordinates create a written list of instructions so that ads, weather, news, public service announcements, and other items follow an exact timetable before broadcast.

During my rocky period at WUSS, when the traffic manager left the station and the position was vacant for thirty days, I volunteered to do traffic along with my other duties for one month. Daily responsibilities returned to normal when a new traffic manager was hired.

I never had an interest in traffic management, but the opportunity to learn enhanced my portfolio. If you can develop a unique skill, you further separate yourself from the masses. Traffic came into play again at WHYY and at NPR. Early on in Philly as operations manager, I transitioned traffic from a word processing-based system to specialized automation software. When the NPR2 traffic manager position was eliminated at NPR, I permanently jumped in to fill that void.

Today, AI, along with automation, is replacing many human-based functions. 'Jack of all trades' opportunities in radio are disappearing. The medium may not have the same doorway to entry-level jobs that my generation had, but audio innovation still survives. Podcasting has matured. Video thrives. Software apps are everywhere. In each sector, audio has a role. Potential radio rookies should look for opportunities and gain experience in all the tangential industries connected to sonic storytelling. If you can't announce behind the microphone, you can write, produce, direct, edit audio and video, or just volunteer to make yourself useful behind the scenes. A jump up front to a more prominent role may come your way after paying some dues and putting in the hard work. Good luck!

Across decades, creative radio talent has always helped the medium reinvent itself when other competing technologies start to chip away at AM and FM's market share. Radio's future will depend on the next generation of innovators who can merge the needs of a changing world with radio's ability to entertain, communicate, and build community. New creators will have broadcast towers, digital systems, and whatever new technologies come along next to hopefully sustain and expand the radio universe to listeners everywhere.

> **"I love to think of nature as an unlimited broadcasting station, through which God speaks to us every hour, if we will only tune in."**
>
> —GEORGE WASHINGTON CARVER

RECOMMENDED READING AND ACKNOWLEDGMENTS

Lots of radio people have compiled comprehensive thoughts about their lives in their craft. You'll find many more examples, but the following books, in alphabetical order, are from my personal library. I highly recommend them to you:

- Jerry Blavat, *You Only Rock Once*, 2011

- Barry Farber, *Making People Talk*, 1987

- Bob Grant, *Let's Be Heard*, 1996

- Hal Jackson with James Haskins, *The House That Jack Built*, 2001

- Larry King, *Larry King by Larry King with Emily Yoffe*, 1982

- John Records Landecker and Rick Kaempfer, *Records Truly Is My Middle Name*, 2013

- Cousin Bruce Morrow and Laura Baudo: *Cousin Brucie: My Life in Rock 'n' Roll Radio*, 1987

- Diane Rehm, *Finding My Voice*, 1999

For the Bigger Picture:

- William Barlow, *Voice Over: The Making of Black Radio*, 1999

- Richard Neer, *FM: The Rise and Fall of Rock Radio*, 2001

- Arnold Passman, *The Deejays: How the Tribal Chieftains of Radio Got to Where They're At*, 1971

- Rick Sklar, *Rocking America: How the All-Hit Radio Stations Took Over*, 1984

To Hear My Airchecks and Artist Interviews:

https://powerhouseradio.com/airchecks

https://youtube.com/@powerhouseradiovideo

Special thanks to Howard Hoffman and Megan Pauly. Very special thanks to Jacqueline Silver-Morillo, CA, Head Reference Librarian/Archivist at the Atlantic City Free Public Library, Atlantic County, New Jersey, and to Mindy Johnson, Principal Librarian, Camden County Library System at the Vogelson Regional Branch, Voorhees, NJ.

BOOKED AND HOOKED ON 5-STAR ARTISTS

B eyond the joy of playing their music, I've enjoyed reading and reviewing many books written by show-stopping entertainers. Across their testimonial pages, secrets are spilled, emotions are bared, and controversies are explained.

From Mary Wilson in 1986 to Janet Jackson in 2011, our proud performers always offer a mouthful of tongue-wagging tales to share. Each of these five book reviews originally appeared as a blog post, as part of a video or as a special website feature that I wrote.

Each book has a co-author, but I don't take off points. A busy musical talent touring worldwide uses their time wisely. Some of these books may have been partially dictated to the co-author, but it doesn't really matter.

Here are my reviews of these five books in chronological order by publication dates.

• • • • •

March, 2004 | *Chaka! Through the Fire*

By Chaka Khan with Tonya Bolden

Review written by Kingsley for the *Powerhouse Radio Newsletter,* March 2004

Released in late 2003, this autobiography tells the personal story of Yvette Stevens, the lady who conquered the music world as Chaka Khan, the 'woman of fire.' Yvette's story starts in Chicago, with lots of detail about her relationship with her mother and father, who were divorced when she was a teenager.

We learn about how the teenage Chaka Khan expressed a new personal awareness through her activities with Chicago's Afro-Arts Theater, and the Black Panther Party.

There's a good balance between feminism, family and music as the reader is introduced to the early artistic stages of this nineteen-time Grammy Award–nominated superstar.

Chaka talks about one of her first teen groups, The Crystalettes, who covered a lot of Top 40 tunes, including Gladys Knight and the Pips, Dionne Warwick and Aretha Franklin. She says, "Yeah, I got a little kick out of being called 'Little Aretha,' but I never wanted to be Aretha. Singing was just a natural thing to do."

Nothing is held back as the story takes off in the early 1970s, when Chaka replaces Paulette McWilliams in Ask Rufus (the group formerly known as The American Breed, whose big hit was "Bend Me, Shape Me").

It's all here—reflections of her friendships with Natalie Cole and Brenda Russell. How Stevie Wonder came up with "Tell Me Something Good" and how Ray Parker Jr. made a valuable contribution to "You Got the Love." Chaka talks candidly about why a friend nicknamed her

Chaka "United Nations" Khan, referencing her spirited relationships with different men from all over the globe.

We share her emotions through an interracial marriage, substance abuse, and her relationship with her children and grandchildren. The book also has an excellent discography arranged chronologically and by album, with sections devoted to her guest appearances, including television and film soundtracks and compilation albums.

Chaka! is an inspiring story everyone should enjoy reading. Published by Rodale Press.

● ● ● ● ●

Donna Summer: Ordinary Girl

By Donna Summer with Marc Eliot

Review written by Kingsley for the *Powerhouse Radio Newsletter,* June, 2004

Donna Summer's autobiography is an enjoyable summer read. LaDonna Adrian Gaines was born on New Year's Eve, December 31, 1948. She grew up in Boston with her parents and two sisters.

By the time she was twelve, she was singing Diana Ross and Dionne Warwick songs. On her approach to singing as an adult, Donna says, "To this day, I will approach a song as an actress approaches a script. I do not sing; I act. When I sing, I sing with the voice of the character in the song."

Referencing Donna's 'act' frame of mind, one can be somewhat forgiving when reflecting on "Love to Love You Baby," her over-the-top exercise in heavy breathing that was a big 1975 disco smash. "Love to Love You Baby" is not one of her personal favorites. Beyonce's "Naughty Girl" brought back the hook from "Love to Love You Baby" in 2003, complete with Donna Summer-styled sensual panting.

By the time she was a teenager, Summer got involved in the cultural revolution that hit the Boston Common section of the city. She auditioned for and got a singing gig with a Blood, Sweat, and Tears-style rock band called The Crow. (Not the same Crow group that had the 1969 hit "Evil Woman, Don't Play No Games with Me.")

She was the witness to a mugging during this period and decided to relocate to New York City to avoid some local Boston hoods.

In the summer of 1968, Donna was living in New York City's Greenwich Village and sharing an apartment with a roommate. One day, her roommate appeared at the apartment with the Broadway producer Bertrand Castelli, who just happened to hear Donna singing while he was outside of the apartment. Donna was invited to audition for the upcoming German production of the new musical *Hair*. She aced the audition. Next, it was off to Germany.

Her story really takes off from here. We share her experiences traveling through Germany and then the rest of Europe as success builds for her theatrical company. Summer's many romances are documented, along with her first marriage to German Helmuth Sommer.

Taking time off after her marriage to have her first child, Donna slowly started getting back into music, picking up singing work wherever she could. A friend told her that producer Giorgio Moroder was looking for new voices for projects in Germany. The two hit it off professionally. Some of Donna's first recordings for Moroder were demos for the group Three Dog Night (to whom Moroder was pitching songs).

By 1973, Summer was recording bubblegum hits in German and making waves in the German top ten. Early in 1975, Donna came up with the concept for "Love to Love You Baby" and gave it to Moroder.

He became so excited about the "Love to Love You Baby" demo that he took the song to MIDEM, an international music festival.

Moroder passed the song on to Neil Bogart of Casablanca Records. One intimate evening, Bogart and his wife played the three-minute demo during an amorous moment. He liked the song so much, he asked Moroder to expand it to eighteen minutes. Now we know why.

Once "Baby" took off, the Donna Summer story relocated to Los Angeles. She leaves Europe and heads back to the USA. As she enters the Hollywood good life, Summer shares with us tales of her bouts with depression, exhaustion, stalkers, ex-lovers, and the usual juicy fare you'd expect from a famous music diva.

From her humble beginning in Boston to triumph, and stormy years in Europe, through ups and downs in LA and New York, to her born-again Christianity, there's a lot that everyone can gain from reading this book. It's a good one.

● ● ● ● ●

Dreamgirl: My Life as a Supreme

By Mary Wilson with Patricia Romanowski and Ahrgus Juilliard

Review written by Kingsley for the *Powerhouse Radio Newsletter* on January 31, 2007

When Mary Wilson, one of the original Supremes, saw the Broadway production of "Dreamgirls" over twenty years ago, she says she was crying by the second act.

> *"I knew in my heart that this story rang far truer than the producers could have imagined." Recently, Motown great Smokey Robinson slammed the movie 'Dreamgirls' for depicting 'false information.'*

*"I was awed at the powerful influence of the Supremes legacy. And
I was more determined than ever that the real story be told."*

With so much controversy surrounding the authenticity of the Dreamgirls movie (even though it is fiction loosely based on fact), let's examine Mary Wilson's side of the story the way she remembers it. Mary ends her version of "Dreamgirls" with emotional reflections revealing her grief over the tragic passing of original Supreme Florence Ballard.

Despite some clear finger-pointing at Diana Ross as the source of competitive tension within the group, once success called, Mary, Diana, and Flo all contributed their share of 'diva madness,' with each lady requiring some high-maintenance 'hand holding.'

The notion that any of the three ladies could have been the ideal lead singer for the group is a theme that Mary focuses on throughout her story.

Ironically, it wasn't until 1964's "Where Did Our Love Go" featuring Diana that the Supremes brought home a hit. They signed with Motown in 1961, initially floundering with songs that failed to click with fans. Most of these tracks were recorded without Diana as the lead vocalist.

Overall, Mary has good things to say about Motown founder Berry Gordy. The 'beyond business' relationship between Gordy and Diana Ross is tastefully told. Wilson provides interesting biographical tidbits about each Motown personality mentioned in the book. Mary debunks myths about Motown's 'Artist Development' department, the folks responsible for grooming, etiquette, and stage polish for the label's acts. Wilson claims that attendance in 'Artist Development' was never mandatory. By today's standards, some of the Supremes 'charm school' 'Artist Development' guidelines seem silly. I got a big laugh when each girl was instructed what to do if another "accidentally picked up her chicken with her fingers."

Mary hammers home first and foremost her belief that the Supremes were a group. Not every member of the quartet (later to become a trio) thought the same way. Strong egos driven by lead singer ambitions strained the professional relationship between Mary and Diana, and Diana and Flo.

However, these teenage friends from Detroit, who would rise to become the dominant female group in the world during a five-year period, had some strong bonds that not even international success could destroy. Mary talks of a strong friendship with Florence Ballard. Wilson indicates how Diana Ross drifted away from very tight spiritual connections with her and Flo Ballard.

Wilson isn't exactly an angel. We get the scoop about her relationship with Duke of the Four Tops (who moved into her house while he was separated from his wife). As a matter of fact, the hanky-panky going on among the various Motown artists is dizzying, as couples pair off during tours, after performances, and after recording sessions.

Mary practically boasts of her long-lasting love affair with the married Tom Jones. Further, she's proud to state, "I had a boyfriend in every town, all around the world. I couldn't wait to meet new people and really enjoy myself." Ms. Wilson tells many amusing stories, including the Beatles' surprise at how "straight-laced" the Supremes appeared during a private gathering in the Fab Four's room at the Warwick Hotel in New York City.

Another great tale is about how two of Diana Ross' dogs munched on some poison outside of the Supremes dressing room at the Latin Casino in Cherry Hill, NJ (June 1969). When the dogs started throwing up, Diana wanted to cancel the two-week, sold-out Supremes engagement.

Mary Wilson succeeds in telling a balanced story about how things really were in the world of the young Detroit dream girls. They blossomed as 'the Primettes' and exploded as 'the Supremes,' reaching new heights in popular music. Between the cat fights, the early struggles, the affairs, the hits, the negative trappings of success, and the fun times on the road, *Dreamgirl: My Life as a Supreme*, according to Mary Wilson, clarifies many of the melodramatic assumptions some say are wildly exaggerated in *Dreamgirls*, the movie.

● ● ● ● ●

Dionne Warwick: My Life as I See It

By Dionne Warwick with David Freeman Wooley

Review written by Kingsley for the *Powerhouse Radio Blog*

February 10, 2011

Dionne Warwick Opens Her Soul in *My Life as I See It*

Dionne Warwick says in her new autobiography, *My Life as I See It*, released in November 2010, that a typo misprint on her first single, "Don't Make Me Over," changed her surname from Warrick to Warwick.

When her astrologer created a numerological chart in the 1970s, the astrologer suggested adding an 'e' to Warwick to create "stronger vibrations." As Dionne says, "that meant every contract, advertisement, and record cover had to reflect the change."

She explains that record sales dipped, so "I went about getting it taken off all contracts, marquees, and future album covers."

My Life as I See It is a very enjoyable read, as Dionne covers every aspect of her life. Her grandfather was a minister. She reflects on how people describe her vocal style as "classical or pop, but gospel has been and always will be first and foremost in my world of music." Dionne Warwick finally released her first gospel album in 2008, *Why We Sing*. She credits gospel with making her a better pop singer.

Here is an artist who spans the decades from the early 1960s to now. She began as a demo track and background singer in New York City, commuting from her home state of New Jersey. When her solo career took off (propelled by songs created by the Hal David, Burt Bacharach writing team), she hit the road to tour. Dionne's stories about experiencing 1963 'Jim Crow' racism traveling through the South echo what my other artists in the early 1960s endured.

Apart from her own talent, Ms. Warwick has glorious singing family connections, including her late sister Dee Dee, aunt Cissy Houston, cousin Whitney Houston, and cousin Leontyne Price.

Excellence takes hard work, and Dionne was no slouch. She took piano lessons every week from age six until her early twenties. When those singers she respected played within a 100-mile radius of one of her performances, she would go to their shows (Lena Horne, Diahann Carroll, and Sammy Davis Jr.) with a legal pad, ask to be seated in the rear of the room with a direct line of sight to the stage, and take notes about every relevant detail of the performance.

She has real bachelor's and master's degrees in music. Dionne speaks frankly about whether her style is Black enough. She says receiving the Rhythm & Blues Foundation Pioneer Award in 2003 was satisfying "to be honored by a sector of the industry that never thought of me as an R&B singer."

> *"My crossover appeal was one of the factors in my success. My music was played on African American stations as well as white radio stations. Ironically, my crossover success in pop prompted*

something that came as a big surprise: the decline of airplay for my
records on African American radio."

When the top New York City R&B station, WWRL, held off adding "Alfie" to their playlist, Warwick recalls that when the song reached the top five position on the *Billboard* R&B charts (and was finally added by the station), she telephoned DJ Rocky G. while he was playing the song and asked, "Why are you playing that white girl's record?" G. answered, "That is no white girl, and who is this?" Dionne's replied, "This is the one you told was too white to play on your show; this is Dionne." The two laughed about that incident for many years to come.

This anecdote reveals the professional aggressiveness that pushes Dionne Warwick forward through a groundbreaking career of many firsts.

- 1968 – First African American since Ella Fitzgerald to win Best Contemporary Pop Vocal Grammy.
- 1979 – First female solo artist to win Grammy awards in pop and R&B in the same year.
- In the 1980s, she was one of the first artists to develop a fragrance, 'Dionne.'
- 1980–1988: She was one of the first African American females to host a music variety television program: Solid Gold (season one and season five).
- *Say a Little Prayer*, her first children's book, was published in 2008.

You get the sense that Dionne Warwick has clear values and is focused, a factor that has contributed to her success.

She talks about embracing collaborations with Barry Manilow, leading to the massive hits "Deja Vu" and "I'll Never Love This Way

Again," but being highly fearful about the "Heartbreaker" song project with the Bee Gees. Dionne explains about several Bee Gees member Barry Gibb songs presented to her: "One I thought was just not me was "Heartbreaker." I did not like it."

Finally giving in to producer Gibb, Ms. Warwick adds, "Needless to say, I was wrong, and he was right. "Heartbreaker" became one of my biggest international hits to date."

I'll close with this Warwick-Mary J. Blige encounter, which gives you further insight into 'the soul of Dionne.' In the 1990s, Warwick participated in organizing talent for a show, *Celebrate the Soul of American Music*.

This program gave her the opportunity "to meet Mary J. Blige. She was 'rough' around the edges at the beginning of her career. But she was an important part of the new sounds that were defining rap and hip-hop."

> *"Why she had been asked to do this show, I don't know, because the Stellar Awards honors the gospel community. But there she was, showing up to rehearse in her fatigues and combat boots. When the dress rehearsal for cameras was about to begin, most artists brought out what they would be wearing to show the colors. Ms. Blige was still in fatigues and combat boots.*

> *"I asked if she would bring out what she intended to wear on the show. In not such a ladylike way, she let me know that she had on what she was going to wear. I had to say that what she had on was not appropriate for the show. I told her I could send one of the stylists out to get her something. But, without missing a beat, she again let me know in no uncertain terms that she was wearing what she had on.*

> *"I then said she would have to wear that somewhere else, because she was no longer on the show. I ran into her again a few years later*

at the inaugural ground-breaking ceremony of the Magic Johnson Theatres in Harlem and I almost didn't recognize her. She was beautifully dressed to the nines. She approached me and asked if I remembered her, and I said I did. She thanked me for opening her eyes to the reality of who she should be and now was.

"Watching her become someone to respect within her community of young entertainers has been great. She is now the epitome of positive imagery and high self-esteem. She has fought the battle with negativity and won the war. Thank you, Mary J. Blige, for being."

And thank you, Dionne Warwick, for an eye-opening book, an amazing career, and your trailblazing pioneer efforts since the early 1960s.

• • • • •

Janet Jackson: True You

By Janet Jackson with David Ritz

Review written by Kingsley for the *Powerhouse Radio Blog*, May 24, 2011

Janet Jackson Is *All True for You*

Inadequate self-esteem resulting from unjustified anxiety. That's the big takeaway from Janet Jackson's 2011 self-help autobiography, *True You*. As Janet describes it, "fear and uncertainty lead to feeling bad about myself."

Along with writer David Ritz, Janet informally details important life transitions that helped her bridge the growth gap between youth and maturity. You won't find a discography of her music in the appendix. You won't find a list of all of her awards.

What *True You* successfully reveals is how the youngest of the famous Jackson siblings finally found independence from certain ingrained family values that ultimately allowed her to break free into a new image, body, career, and love comfort zone. *True You* is surprisingly different from the expected 'tell all' tone of other bios, written by music celebrities, who usually attract readers by sharing seedy tabloid tales.

I like how Janet strategically incorporates some powerful fan letters into her own story to illuminate universal themes of struggle, hurt, pain, and loss. This book is dedicated to her late brother, Michael. Janet talks vibrantly about their special, close relationship. Down-to-earth details document siblings who are not hung up on their celebrity.

Janet relates fond memories about her youngest years with 'Mike.' Michael would repeatedly drive the two to different Los Angeles fast food restaurants, buy lots of goodies, and then go to areas in the city populated by the homeless to distribute the food.

Food fables dominate *True You*. Janet's battle of the bulge is well documented, including her 2008 drop from 180 to 120 pounds. A lifetime of eating and yo-yo dieting are the outcomes of Janet's sensitive personality, as she would react to teasing, criticism, and professional demands by turning to food.

I enjoyed the afterword: "It's Not a Diet," written by her nutritionist, David Allen, who, in analyzing their long-term interactions, stresses that changes in lifestyle, balanced meals, and adequate sleep were crucial in order for Janet to reach her goals.

True You closes with nearly eighty pages of recipes designed by Janet Jackson and cooked for her by Chef Andre. Some of the suggestions detail the preparation of 'Veggie Baked Eggs' (kid-friendly), 'Baked Oven Fries,' and 'Honey Yogurt with Peaches and Toasted Almond Parfait.'

Janet ends her self-help autobiography story with these words of guidance:

"Proper nutrition"

"Restorative sleep"

"Wholesome foods"

"Self-care, physically, mentally, emotionally, and spiritually."

Bravo, Janet. Sunshine with plenty of warmth beams through *True You*. Nasty!

● ● ● ● ●

Note: When a documentary about Janet Jackson appeared on *Lifetime* and *A&E* television in 2022, I used this written review to create a YouTube video.

PHOTO GALLERY

Thirteen, and having fun in the cafeteria. I'm in the ninth grade, 1965.
The blazer was part of the high school dress code *(L. Jefferson Siegel).*

With Mom, Mildred A. Smith in August, 1983 (*private collection*).

On the Long John Nebel Show at 66 WNBC Radio in New York City.
October, 1968. I'm a senior in high school. (*L. Jefferson Siegel*).

Filling in for Al Roberts at **WBLS FM NYC**, spring 1974 (*private collection*).

In the studio at **WNYU AM FM** New York University 1974 (*private collection*).

With WHUR FM's Robyn Holden at WHUR FM, Washington, DC September, 1976 . Two years earlier we were both part of the original WUSS Atlantic City on-air staff (*private collection*).

The 1976 WUSS AM Atlantic City, NJ on-air staff holding our gold records. Ron King, Elana Van Skii, Bobby Jay, Kingsley, John Hand, Ansel Vee, Robbie Long, Cleo Rowe (*private collection*).

Drummer Harvey Mason at WUSS after our 1976 on-air interview (*Corney Bell*).

Kingsley, Cleo Rowe, Ben E. King, and Chuck Clark at
Arthurs, Atlantic City, NJ in 1977 (*private collection*).

Snookie Jones, RCA Records, Carrie Lucas, A.J. Kemp WDAS FM,
Kingsley in 1979 at Second Story, Philadelphia, PA (*Scott Weiner*).

Stephanie Mills, Kingsley, Diane Prior, evening host at
WAYV FM, Atlantic City, 1980 (*Snookie Jones*).

Phyllis Hyman after her Atlantic City Boardwalk Hall concert in 1981. I introduced her and brought her on stage. Phyllis
was a tall one. She's siting in a chair! R.I.P. (*private collection*).

THE

Z106
ALL HIT RADIO
WZGO
1985
MUSIC
SURVEY!

HAPPY HOLIDAYS FROM THE ENTIRE Z-106 CREW! Top Row: Wes Heywood, Andre Gardner; Second Row: David Blaise, Nancy Leigh, Ross Brittain, Kingsley Smith, Matt Farber, Steve Davis, Chris Trane; Front Row: Traci Becker, Cynthia Weber, Harriet Coffey.

No other Philadelphia radio station gave away more cash and more prizes in 1985...and the winning is just beginning!

THE Z106 1985 COUNTDOWN CONTEST!
LISTEN AND WIN!

POWER EVENTS

Every Wednesday
Frank Cerami's 70's Dance Party
at Glitters.
427 South Street

We Put It On Our Bumper and Won!

Pictured (L-R) Tony Q, Program Director, Donna Basford, winner from Camden, NJ, afternoon jock Mike Love, Jackie Singleton, winner from West Philly, POWER staffer Mary Renkiewicz (with Singleton's daughter). In the forefront (L-R) jocks Don "Juan" Banks and Kingsley Smith. Both Donna and Jackie were winners in POWER 99fm/Dodge Daytona Giveway!

POWER 99fm — The Station That Doubles The Winnings!

1986 WUSL, Philadelphia a.k.a. Power 99 fm.

At the Public Radio Program Director's Conference, 1992 with Afropop Worldwide host Georges Collinet (*private collection*).

In the television studio, WHYY TV 12 in Philadelphia, WHYY 90.9 FM's sister station. *Voices in the Family* radio host Dr. Dan Gottlieb Ph.D. center, and Radio Manager Mark Vogelzang, 1992 (*private collection*).

In the studio with India.Arie after she appeared on NPR's
Talk of The Nation in 2006 (*private collection*).

Live on-air during NPR's *Morning Edition* raising money for NPR FM Berlin in
the NPR Washington, DC studio. Joining me is WAMU FM Washington, DC
Hot Jazz Saturday Night host Rob Bamberger. January 2014 (*private collection*).

Kingsley, NPR President and CEO Jarl Mohn, Alex Curley, Associate Producer/Director, and intern Angelica Dennis outside of NPR Washington, DC headquarters in 2015 (*private collection*).

With Verdine White, Olivia Burton, Philip Bailey, Kingsley, and Ralph Johnson. Earth, Wind & Fire - Chicago concert in Camden, New Jersey (*private collection*).

Flavor Flav at Kelsey's in Atlantic City, NJ before a Boardwalk
Hall Legends of Hip Hop concert in January, 2015 that featured Public Enemy and other performers (*private collection*).

In the home studio, 2015.

NOTES

1   Federal Communications Commission, *Statement of Policy on Minority Ownership of Broadcasting Facilities*, 78-322 95lll, Washington, D.C.: GPO, FCC, 1978, https://www.fcc.gov/document/statement-policy-minority-ownership-broadcasting-facilities.

2   Federal Communications Commission, *Statement of Policy on Minority Ownership of Broadcasting Facilities.*

3   Federal Communications Commission, *Statement of Policy on Minority Ownership of Broadcasting Facilities.*

4   Federal Communications Commission, *Statement of Policy on Minority Ownership of Broadcasting Facilities.*

5   Federal Communications Commission, *Telecommunications Act of 1996*, S.652 - 104th Congress, Washington, D.C.: GPO, FCC, 1996, https://www.fcc.gov/general/telecommunications-act-1996.

6   American Research Bureau, *Audience Measurement*, 1974.

7   Philip Greer and Myron Kandel, "Black Radio Network Reaches for Big Advertising Dollars," In The Marketplace (column), newspaper unknown, 1978.

8   "WUSS Boss: 3 Whites, 2 Blacks Fired," *Press of Atlantic City*,

July 11, 1975.

9   New Jersey Statues, *New Jersey Casino Control Act*, N.J.S.A. 5, Trenton, NJ, 1977, https://www.nj.gov/casinos/law/gaming-nj.

10   Federal Communications Commission, *Consumer Guide Payola Rules*, 47 U.S.C. § 317, Washington, D.C.: GPO, FCC, 2017, https://www.fcc.gov/sites/default/files/payola-rules.pdf.

11   "Jersey Radio Station Struck," *New York Times*, December 3, 1977.

12   "Quality Listening Via WAYV," *Press of Atlantic City*, October 16, 1976.

13   Federal Communications Commission, *FCC Eliminates the Duplication Rule for AM and FM Radio Stations*, FCC-20-109, Washington, D.C.: GPO, FCC, 2020, https://www.fcc.gov/document/fcc-eliminates-duplication-rule-am-and-fm-radio-stations.

14   Federal Communications Commission, *FCC Eliminates the Duplication Rule for AM and FM Radio Stations*.

15   The Arbitron Company, *Arbitron Radio: Audience Estimates*, (Atlantic City, NJ: Arbitron, 1979).

16   The Arbitron Company, *Radio Terms for the Trade*, (Arbitron, 1996).

17   The Arbitron Company, *Arbitron Radio: Audience Estimates*, (Atlantic City, NJ: Arbitron, 1980.)

18   Mikala Lugenjul, "The Day Disco Died: Remembering the Unbridled Chaos of Disco Demolition Night," EDM.com, July 12, 2021, https://edm.com/features/remembering-disco-demolition-night-1979.

19   Barbara Faggins, "Jim Wade has Just Begun to Strut his Stuff." *Philadelphia Tribune*, September 4, 1981.

20   Kevin Riordan, "WSSJ Lights up Dial with 'City Rhythm.'"

Courier Post, September 3, 1981.

21 Marc Sugarman, "Soundtracks," *Jewish Exponent*, February 25, 1983.

22 "Carroll to Consult WIFI," Radio & Records, February 11, 1983, https://worldradiohistory.com/Archive-All-Music/Archive-RandR/1980s/1983/RR-1983-02-11.pdf.

23 "NPR's Drive to Survive," NPR Historical Archives, NPR.org, August, 1983, https://www.npr.org/2021/04/28/987733236/a-timeline-of-nprs-first-50-years.

24 Corporation for Public Broadcasting, "CPB Saves NPR from Bankruptcy," CPB.org History Timeline, August 2, 1983, https://cpb.org/AboutCPB/History-Timeline.

25 Corporation for Public Broadcasting, "About CPB," CPB.org, https://cpb.org/aboutcpb.

26 Amy Webb, "The Cost to Know WHYY," *Philadelphia City Paper*, July 8 – 14, 2004, https://mycitypaper.com/articles/2004-07-08/cover.shtml.

27 Mark Rohland and Kingsley Smith, "Where Has All the Radio Gone?," *Philadelphia Inquirer*, January 12, 1998.

28 Cox Communications, Inc., *Look Who's Back in Philadelphia Consulting for Z106*, (Philadelphia, PA: Cox, 1986).

29 U.S. Copyright Office, *The Digital Millennium Copyright Act*, H.R.2281 105th Congress (1997-1998), Washington, D.C.:GPO, 1998, https://www.copyright.gov/dmca.

30 Michelle Ruoff, "DMCA Compliance," Live365.org, January 27, 2017, https://live365.com/blog/broadcaster/dmca-compliance.

31 "NPR Stations and Public Media," NPR.org, 2023, https://www.npr.org/about-npr/178640915/npr-stations-and-public-media.

32   Eric J. Savitz, "SiriusXM Shares Tumble on Disappointing 2023 Outlook," *Barron's*, February 2, 2023, https://www.barrons.com/articles/siriusxm-shares-tumble-on-disappointing-2023-outlook-51675353327.

33   Shirley Huang, "Sirius XM Radio to Announce Full Year and Fourth Quarter 2012 Results," SiriusXM, January 17, 2013, https://investor.siriusxm.com/news-events/press-releases/detail/158/sirius-xm-radio-to-announce-full-year-and-fourth-quarter.

34   Edison Research, *The Infinite Dial*, 2023, https://www.edison-research.com/wp-content/uploads/2023/03/The-Infinite-Dial-2023.pdf.

35   Voice of America, "VOA Through the Years," *VOA Public Relations*, April 03, 2017, https://www.insidevoa.com/a/3794247.html.

36   Voice of America, "The VOA Charter," *VOA Archive*, October 30, 2009, https://www.voanews.com/a/a-13-a-2003-06-06-41-1/298770.html.

37   Nette Nöstlinger, "America's Voice Goes Silent in Berlin as Last US Radio Station Closes." *Politico*, December 29, 2020, https://www.politico.eu/article/us-radio-station-kcrw-berlin-closes.

38   Clint C. Wilson II, *Whither the Black Press?: Glorious Past, Uncertain Future* (Indiana: Xlibris LLC, 2014), 129.

39   Public Radio Program Directors Association, *"Core Values,"* PRPD, 2000, https://prpd.org/resources/core-values.

40   Public Radio Program Directors Association, *"Core Values."*

41   "No One Wants to Leave Home; PRPD, PBS Cancel Meetings," *Current*, September 24, 2001, https://current.org/wp-content/uploads/archive-site/pb/pb0117terror.html.

42   Tim Karr, "Why NPR's Layoffs Are a Public Policy Problem." *Common Dreams*, February 25, 2023, https://www.common-

dreams.org/opinion/npr-layoffs-funding-public-media.

43 World Book Encyclopedia Dictionary, 'Per capita'. *World Book Encyclopedia Dictionary*, Doubleday & Company, Inc., 1963.

44 Corporation for Public Broadcasting, "*Why does public broadcasting need federal funding?*," CPB, https://cpb.org/faq#1-3.

45 KUT 90.5 and KUTX 98.9, "CPB Funding Overview," KUT, 2021 https://www.kut.org/cpb-funding-overview.

46 Snoadmin, "Money Worries for KCRW," Corsair, March 14, 2011, https://www.thecorsaironline.com/corsair/news/2011/03/15/money-worries-for-kcrw.

47 Maine Public. "Facts About Maine Public's Federal Funding," Maine Public Radio, 2022, https://www.mainepublic.org/facts-about-maine-publics-federal-funding.

48 WHYY, "Financial Statements." WHYY, 2022, https://whyy.org/financial-statements.

49 Arizona PBS. "Support Arizona PBS." Arizona PBS, 2023, https://azpbs.org/support.

50 Federal Communications Commission, *EAS Emergency Alert System*, FCC, Washington, D.C.: GPO, 2007, https://docs.fcc.gov/public/attachments/DOC-278628A5.pdf.

INDEX